RECHARGE

Lessons to **revitalise yourself, your team** or **your business** in *60 minutes or less*

Alan Hargreaves

Wrightbooks

For my father

First published 2011 by Wrightbooks
an imprint of John Wiley & Sons Australia, Ltd
42 McDougall Street, Milton Qld 4064

Office also in Melbourne

Typeset in Berkeley LT 11.3/14.5pt

© Alan Hargreaves 2011

The moral rights of the author have been asserted

National Library of Australia Cataloguing-in-Publication entry

Author:	Hargreaves, Alan.
Title:	Recharge: how to revitalise yourself, your team or your business in 60 minutes or less / Alan Hargreaves.
ISBN:	9780730375203 (pbk.)
Notes:	Includes index.
Subjects:	Success in business.
	Self-actualization (Psychology)
	Employee motivation.
	Organizational effectiveness.
Dewey Number:	658.314

Cover image: iStockphoto.com/© DSGpro

Cover design by Peter Reardon, Pipeline Design <www.pipelinedesign.com.au>

Printed in China by Printplus Limited

10 9 8 7 6 5 4 3 2 1

Disclaimer
The material in this publication is of the nature of general comment only, and does not represent professional advice. It is not intended to provide specific guidance for particular circumstances and it should not be relied on as the basis for any decision to take action or not take action on any matter which it covers. Readers should obtain professional advice where appropriate, before making any such decision. To the maximum extent permitted by law, the author and publisher disclaim all responsibility and liability to any person, arising directly or indirectly from any person taking or not taking action based upon the information in this publication.

Contents

Contents

About the author

Alan Hargreaves has spent 35 years in financial services and business consulting. His approach to management is highly effective, yet inspiringly simple. It focuses on real issues rather than strategic principles. His mix of personal and collaborative action brings immediate traction.

After completing an economics degree at the University of Sydney, Alan worked for 20 years in international finance. He has built businesses in Hong Kong, Singapore and New York. Since returning to Australia in 1998, he has managed his own private investment trust.

Alan has worked extensively with business audiences through both radio and television. His private equity and advisory services span IT, media, property, finance, communications and retail. He is regularly engaged as a speaker, consultant and mentor. His passions are business, boats and breeding horses.

Acknowledgements

This book has been a long time coming. It is the result of support and encouragement from an enormous number of people over many years. Some are family and business colleagues; others are consulting clients or friends. Many are both. Some, like my mother and father, are no longer with us. I thank them all. Collectively they provided the experiences and support that enabled me to conceive the project and finish it, even if they don't know it.

In particular, I owe a debt to my monthly think tank: David Norman, Bob Burns, Kris Barkway and David Turner. They prompted the idea. Thanks also to those who read the manuscript and gave such great feedback: Yvonne Collier, who does not have the word 'negative' in her vocabulary; Sean Urquhart, who pointed out sins of omission in sections on finance; and to Greg Power who made me feel that I actually understood some things about marketing.

A conversation with Andrew Griffiths was the turning point. He inspired me to carry on with the project when I was almost ready to shelve it. He also introduced me to my agent, Carolyn Crowther, who had the temerity to suggest I try to publish it, and who helped me turn some turgid copy into what I hope are now readable chapters. My copy editor, Robyn Wilkie, introduced me to the idea of grammar—a concept I found quite novel. She deserves thanks for her perseverance, as do all the members of the editorial team at John Wiley & Sons.

None of this would have happened without my family. And my family would not have happened without Lesley, my wife and partner of 40 years. No editorial slouch, she has the ability to spot a typo at 20 paces. She also has the uncanny knack of suggesting alternative phraseology without destroying my ego in the process.

Nonetheless, any shortcomings that remain can only be ascribed to me. The first draft is now a long way behind. The extent to which this book is an improvement on the original is thanks to all who have so graciously assisted me in the process.

Introduction

How good does it feel when your business hums? Or when your career is on a roll? There's a real excitement. The train has left the station and you are on it. You may not know where it is going, and even that is exhilarating. You don't mind turning up at all. You look forward to the next day before it has started. The mood is infectious. Your colleagues are pleased to see you walk in and you are glad to be working with them. You love your team. They like your energy and your stream of new ideas, even the stupid ones. They have plenty of ideas too. All of you know that you are building something together. There's continuous action and a sense of momentum. That's what a fully charged business feels like.

How's yours? What action are you taking to get on that roll? It doesn't take a major strategic overhaul to start moving. You are surrounded by opportunities to recharge your business. You just need to look.

I learned this in a car park. When I was halfway through hitchhiking around Australia, I was parking cars in an abandoned warehouse in Adelaide. Our 95 car spaces were full from Monday to Friday, but on Saturday we'd be lucky to fill 30. The boss, known as 'Old Jack', decided to take off Saturdays. He had me run that shift and have Mondays off instead. The Saturday shift was a drag. I hated it. Yet it was here I learned one of the first rules of business: it works better when you're busy. It doesn't really matter what the action is, just take some. The shift will be shorter if you do.

I offered to wash cars. I told Jack I'd split the proceeds 50:50 with him. He was okay with that and I needed the cash. From then on, I asked everyone who drove in if they wanted a wash. Not much happened, but when I put a sandwich board out the front, things started to build. That was a little bit exciting. I wondered what else I could do. I asked some regulars about the Saturday problem and they told me our weekend prices were too high. I told Jack we could probably fill more spaces if we lowered our prices. He said to give it a go. The next week our sandwich board advertised in large letters our 'Shopper's Special'. Because of the car wash and the price change, our Saturday numbers started to creep and were soon over 50.

Then more people wanted car washes, and we were becoming backed up. I told Jack, and he offered the weekday staff a weekend washing shift. They needed some extra dollars too. Once we did that, things started to hum. More people came in for the wash only, and we charged a higher price for that. I started to look forward to Saturdays. Our target was to fill the car park. We kept score on a blackboard. I smiled every time a customer drove in. I still remember the day we reached our target. We had to create space for a few more cars by cleaning up the back alley and having an old wreck towed away. Jack was happy. He still didn't have to turn up on Saturdays and he was making more money. So were we.

What had happened? Nothing more than a little action. We didn't call any of these things 'initiatives'. I didn't suggest to Jack that we diversify our product offering, or tell him that our customer focus group recommended we realign our pricing structure. We didn't review our fixed asset base and eliminate legacy items to free up resources. No-one suggested we introduce an incentive element into the remuneration policy or explore new avenues in display marketing. We just took a little action. That led to more action. Gradually everything started to lift.

That's what this book is about: taking a little action. Sometimes that can lead to very big actions, and to projects that hum louder than a rock concert. But you won't achieve this without taking the first step.

That's what I did in Adelaide. I had partied too hard in my first year of university, failed three out of four subjects, lost my scholarship, crashed my mother's car and dropped out. Of course, I thought I was a legend, but I knew my batteries were low. I needed a recharge and I found one at Jack's parking garage. Action created action. A few months later I left Adelaide, jumped on a freight train and headed west to the nickel boom. By the end of the year I had saved enough to return to Sydney and re-enrol in university. This time I sailed through.

Do you need a recharge? Most people do. I know I have to shake things up every couple of years. Some of the most talented people I deal with manage to stagnate every now and then. They include gifted entrepreneurs who have created great businesses but suddenly lose momentum when they have to *run* the businesses. I also know brilliant salespeople who have advanced from head of marketing to managing director in a flash, but then stall. What do they do now?

They can start by reading this book.

It's very easy. There are 52 chapters. That's one a week. You can read and digest every one in less than an hour. Each chapter points to an action you can take to start moving. There's no complicated management-speak. Just plain English and simple ideas you can put into practice with a minimum of fuss. *Recharge* is for people who run their own businesses and are serious about success. It is also for people who run someone else's business and are serious about their careers. It was written to stimulate action. As economists tell us, the best way out of depression is stimulus. It's the same in business management. Start with the first chapter and start now. It's time for action.

PART I

Recharge yourself

'Recharge yourself' sets up your management platform. Simple processes will help you get on track and moving forward. They will clear away dysfunctional elements in your working environment and give you a clean launching pad for taking action. You will identify your own strengths and will be challenged to use them firmly and effectively. You will learn strategies to boost your standing both within your industry and within your firm. You will be prompted to collaborate with others in ways that leverage your management skills. Step-by-step instructions will guide you through handling difficult situations, giving you the clarity, strength and openness to handle the broad range of issues this book addresses.

1
Mission, strategy and action
Does anyone know why businesses work?

Great effort goes into business thinking, yet little seems to change. Businesses still open and close. Major corporations are deemed excellent one decade, but decline in the next. Last year's best practice is quickly eclipsed by the latest trend. Some studies say most new businesses fail within five years.

What actually makes a business work well? Plenty of commentators claim to have identified the essential ingredients of business success, whether for large corporations or for smaller enterprises or for both. Is any of this information really useful? And if it is, just how complicated does it need to be?

In *The Halo Effect*, Phil Rosenzweig's critique of business theory, we find notions that have become accepted benchmarks for achieving success. The list includes lofty and often commendable phrases: 'customer focus', 'entrepreneurial culture', 'clear vision', 'flawless execution' and 'performance orientation'. And there are glib slogans that now seem permanently parked in management terminology: 'sticking to the knitting', being 'hands-on', 'managing by walking around' and even setting 'big hairy audacious goals'. Rosenzweig's view is not so much that all these clichés are incorrect or ineffective. Rather, they are either the characteristics you would expect to find in a successful business, or they are business practices that a successful corporation can afford to implement. Or possibly both.

The point is that many businesses aim for, and actually achieve, practices that incorporate these ideas, yet not all of them are successful. In other words, the authors of many business classics have simply examined successful

2

organisations and listed their characteristics. However, it is important to remember that correlation is not causation. That is, just because successful firms *have* these characteristics, it does not mean those characteristics *made* them successful. There seem to be an enormous number of businesses that have succeeded in spite of themselves. In some cases, it's thanks to forces outside their control. In others, it's due to developments that could not be foreseen, let alone identified well in advance in a strategic plan based on business theory. However, a common element of successful businesses is a preparedness to take action.

Anyone who has read Richard Branson's autobiography will know that the creation of Virgin Records was hardly a carefully planned sequence of events. At times, the Virgin empire seemed to lurch from one crisis to another. But, crucially, the firm was prepared to take action—often quite drastic action.

All that most businesspeople—successful or otherwise—appear to have in common is that they:

▷ started a business (Branson began with an unprofitable student newspaper)
▷ were reasonably well organised (questionable in Branson's early days)
▷ got on with the job (probably Branson's strongest suit).

Too simplistic? Not really. These are three very simple prerequisites for turning your vision into business success. First, you have to actually get started—you have to put your vision into practice. Second, you have to plan your business so that the mission can be achieved. In other words, you have to be reasonably well organised. Third, you have to take the necessary actions to implement the plan. It doesn't mean you will be successful, but it ensures you will implement something—and that something will be operating in the market when (or if) success comes.

Success rarely follows a formula. Timing and luck will always play a part. This is what business risk is about. You may be able to take steps to curb the risk of a change in conditions, or, alternatively, to take advantage of it. But you cannot eliminate it.

How do you find the right perspective?

Cut through the jargon by looking at the basic components of a business. There are shareholders (who provide the money), directors (who decide on the plan) and managers (who implement the plan). In a sole proprietorship, you are all three. In a large corporation, you might be one or two, and sometimes all three. Whichever hat you are wearing, you need to be clear about your role. Start with shareholders.

Shareholders: the mission

Shareholders provide the mission, and it is simple: to optimise returns for shareholders over time. The vision may be anything. It may be to invest in green products. It may be to plough all profits into preferred industries. It may even be a not-for-profit business if that is what the shareholders want. The mission, however, is to optimise the return they want.

The mission does not change. In figures 1.1, 1.2 (overleaf) and 1.3 (p. 8), it is represented by the thick, black line. In the last few centuries, it hasn't shifted. It is constant over time and will continue to be so in the future.

A lot of effort is devoted to designing fashionable mission statements. It can be time well spent. But these statements are more to do with the culture of the firm, or strategies to fulfil the mission—things like 'being the preferred supplier in sector M' or 'maintaining best practice in quality management'. They are all useful, but they are secondary to your mission. For our purposes, your mission is a given. Even if the environment in which you operate is shifting dramatically, your mission is unchanged: it is to optimise the return for your shareholders over time. You may be the only shareholder or there may be many. But the mission remains the same.

Figure 1.1: shareholders' mission

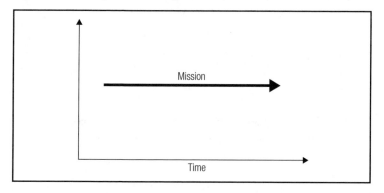

Directors: strategy and planning

That brings us to strategy and planning. This is where it can become messy. Planning how to achieve the mission can be confusing. There are strategic plans, business plans and implementation plans. All are useful. You cannot go to where you want to be without a road map.

Directors sit in the middle. There is creative tension here. On one hand, they have to work on behalf of shareholders to develop a strategy to fulfil the mission; on the other, they have to work with managers to produce a business plan that implements the strategy.

Let's be clear about the difference between the *strategic plan* and the *business plan*.

Strategy is about the big questions: Where is the business heading over the long term? How should it adapt to expected changes in the business environment? What core values should sit beneath its method of operation? These are all important issues.

The problem with strategic plans is that they are often slow to change. In a dynamic environment, the use-by date of a strategic plan starts approaching the moment the plan is completed. Unlike the mission, these plans have no inherent longevity. Over time, and as the business environment changes, the efficacy of the strategic plan—its ability to fulfil the mission—gradually decreases.

The line XX in figure 1.2 shows this relationship. Firms evolve. They don't remain static. They adapt or die. Strategy has a place, but it needs to be dynamic. The directors need to maintain a strategic dialogue rather than stick rigidly to a view that exists at only one point in time.

Figure 1.2: shareholders' mission and strategic planning

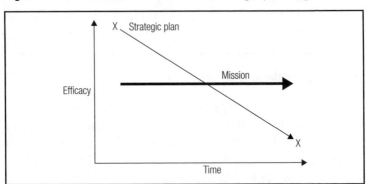

In the meantime, you have to run the business and maintain its performance. That is where the business plan comes in. It is necessarily more flexible, because if something is not working, you need to change it quickly. It is still a road map, but it must be capable of making detours. The more straightforward the plan, the more effective it will be. Directors can't work in isolation here. They need to collaborate with managers to create a business plan that is motivating, achievable, robust and flexible.

It need not be complicated. Most businesses are simple. They invest an amount (capital) to set up operations to create a product or service at a cost, then the product or service is sold to a target market. This is the case for any business, large or small.

The business plan then needs to address each step:

1 How much capital will be needed and how will it be applied?
2 What operations and people need to be put in place?
3 What are the qualities of the product or service?
4 What will it cost to run the business?
5 Can enough of the output be sold at a price that covers the costs?
6 Who is the target market and how will you sell to them?

If you wish to spend more time on this, your search engine will guide you to numerous free templates for putting together a plan. Most will address the above list in one form or another. In any case, a guide to preparing one is available at <www. alanhargreaves.com>. At this point, however, we are more concerned with prompting management momentum rather than planning for it. It is why you have to be reasonably well organised rather than highly organised. This brings us to the manager.

Managers: implementation and action

Business plans need to be theoretically stress-tested, but they are usually common sense. Most managers have a clear idea of what needs to be done. The main use of the plan is to clearly specify the tasks that have to be carried out, by whom and by when. Few businesses move from A to B in a straight line. Management decisions along the way ensure that plans are implemented and momentum is maintained.

That is why the primary focus of this book is on managers. These are the people at the coalface. They know what the mission is. They know what the plan is. They have to make it work. To do so, they have to be dynamic and creative.

Rather than sticking rigidly to a static plan, managers have to be highly adaptive. The importance of this ability to adapt and take action is shown in the line YY in figure 1.3. The role of management action does not decrease over time. Rather, it becomes more important. Richard Branson may not be the perfect role model for your situation, but his strength in this area is a core element in Virgin's success.

Unlike strategic plans, managers can respond quickly. Their role is at a premium when the environment is shifting. It is essential that they are able to see the whole picture. That is why this book takes a holistic view of the firm. Managers need to understand the key principles behind the entire spectrum of business operations and be ready to act appropriately. You may not have any experience in marketing, but you need to know its basic principles. The same is true for finance or running a team in an area you know nothing about.

Figure 1.3: mission, strategic planning and management

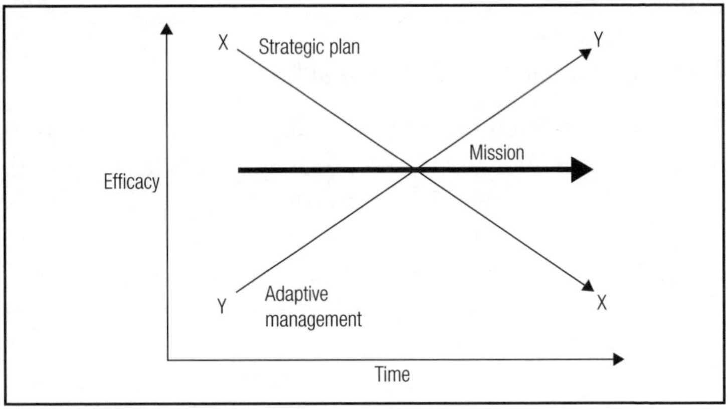

Remember the roles

Across their careers, even possibly at the same time, most managers will be required to wear all three hats—shareholder, director and manager. Regardless of where you are now, keep a clear view of what is required of each, because they all have an impact on one another.

➤ As a *shareholder*, you need to be clear about what you expect from your investment. Regardless of your vision, you want an optimal return on your shareholding. Even if you are the only shareholder, you need to know what you want that return to be and over what time horizon. If you are not a shareholder, understand that return on investment is still the mission. You will be rewarded by the extent to which it is fulfilled.

➤ As a *director*, you must develop the firm's strategic and business plans. The strategies reflect the mission; the business plan implements the strategy. The plans must be manageable, and the managers must be empowered to manage. You are responsible for this either as a sole director or as a member of a board of directors.

➤ As a *manager*, you have to implement the plan. The more flexible, imaginative, action-oriented and knowledgeable you are, the more likely it is that you will be able to bring together the mission, the plan and its implementation. The successful firm requires all three. Figure 1.3 illustrates the balance of these elements.

In the next chapter, we will start to take action. But before we go there, do this simple exercise.

Try on each hat. Sit on three different chairs if you like. On the first — the shareholders' chair — spend a few quiet minutes understanding and acknowledging the central importance of the mission and what it means for your business. On the next — the director's chair — think about the strategic and business plans you are charged with creating. Visualise their achievement. On the last — the manager's chair — think of yourself as an action figure. How will you handle what lies ahead? You are the one who is going to make this happen.

2 Begin with some simple action

A first step towards prioritising

This will take 25 minutes.

Today, you need to take some simple action. In later chapters, you will look at specific business issues, but right now you need to check your priorities. What are the things you want to work on, or need to work on? Are any things *not* working for you? You need to do something about them right away. You don't need to compile an exhaustive 'to do' list. That would take more time to work up than it would to work out. You need to identify some things you can act on now. This is about small steps, not running the marathon.

Personal balance

In table 2.1, you will find a personal balance assessment worksheet. This is a straightforward template. You can draw it on any sheet of paper. (If you prefer something more formal, download the template and instructions from <www.alanhargreaves.com>. It's free.)

The worksheet lists seven different areas of everyday life. The areas covered are not exhaustive, but they encompass most of the aspects of our lives. They are like spokes in a wheel. Some strength or focus on each one is required to keep the wheel balanced. There will be times when one area is more important than others, but none can be ignored entirely. This process aims to focus your attention on areas where action now would bring greatest benefit and on areas in which some effort is required to restore balance.

Table 2.1: personal balance assessment

Areas	Now (A)	Goal (B)	Rank (B – A)	Positives (your strengths in this area)	Action (what could help achieve your goal)
Health and fitness					
Career and business					
Financial security					
Personal growth					
Intimate relationships					
Community					
Recreation and leisure					

You will rate your current performance in each area using a number in the range of 1 (lowest score) to 10 (highest score). But first, familiarise yourself with each area and get a feel for what each one entails. The following paragraphs might assist in stimulating your thoughts.

Health and fitness

Few people score 10 in this area. Many healthy people desire improvements in their fitness or changes in their lifestyle. They may want to stop smoking, drink less, run more, lose weight, put on weight, recover from injury or illness or address emotional and mental issues that are holding them back. Maybe they just want more rest or to schedule idle, stress-free time. Or read a book.

How do you feel about your health and fitness right now?

Career and business

Is your career progressing well? Is it taking you where you want to go? Are you taking it where you want to go? Do you want to get there faster? Are you in the right business? Do you want to be in business at all? Do you lack skills that would improve your score? Do you feel disorganised or unmotivated? Is there a project or objective you want to achieve more quickly? Do you like your work environment? Do you want a fundamental change in this area? Are you planning a change in employer or industry?

How do you feel about your career or business right now?

Financial security

This is a tough one. Legend has it that when asked 'How much is enough?', John D Rockefeller answered, 'A little bit more'. Very few people accept their financial condition, be it excellent or poor. What exactly is your goal? And where do you stand now relative to that goal? What is required to achieve your goal? Is it realistic? Would you just like to stop worrying about it and move on with your life? Do you have specific financial difficulties that you need to address? What is going right, financially? What financial things do you do well?

How do you feel about your financial security right now?

Personal growth

Are you developing as a person? Do you need to? Are you fine the way you are? Really? Personal growth can mean many things to different people. Do you feel underqualified? Is there anything you can do about it? Do you have personal issues that you need to resolve? Do you want to develop spiritually? How is your mental health? Your anger? Do you want to be calmer, or more active? Do you think there is more change, development or personal growth ahead of you, or have you peaked?

How do you feel about your personal growth right now?

Intimate relationships

This area can include any relationship that matters to you. It could be with your spouse, children, extended family, friends, boss, work colleagues, neighbours—just about anyone. Are any not working? Can you pinpoint why?

How do you feel about your relationships with other people right now?

Community

How do you interact with your community—do you help at a school, church, sporting group, charity, club or pub? Do you avoid your community? Does lack of involvement limit your choices or curb your opportunities? Do you like it that way? Why?

How do you feel about your participation in the community right now?

Recreation and leisure

Remember that recreation and leisure, no matter how defined, can play a crucial role in maintaining a balanced life. It may be that you just want to play more golf. Or less.

How do you rate the part that recreation and leisure play in your life right now?

Complete the personal balance assessment

The worksheet for this process is provided in table 2.1 (p. 11). However, you can simply draw your own. You might like to work with someone else on the process. Have them do it too. This will spark more ideas than you will have on your own. Work through the areas using the following guidelines.

Now

In the column headed 'Now', quickly rate your current performance in each area by choosing a number from 1 (poor) to 10 (excellent). Do not dwell on this. The first number that comes into your head is likely to be very close to the mark. Do not be concerned that some of the areas do not feel of importance to you. Just rate yourself in the category and move on to the next.

Positives

Skip across to the column headed 'Positives'. In this column, list at least one (but no more than three) strengths that you have in this area. There is no zero in this template. The lowest you can score is 1. That's because you must have some capability, natural talent or skill in each area (even in areas that are not your strongest suits). Maybe you are just not using these at the moment. If you scored only 1, think about what helped you achieve that score. Scoring only 2, for example, might look like poor performance, but something helped you achieve a 2. What was it?

Goal

In this column, write down the level at which you would like to perform in each area. This doesn't always have to be an advance. Many people are happy with their career development or the state of their business. Others aren't. Some gym junkies would like to cut back their training sessions but find they just can't. However, there will be other places where you feel you would like to see some improvement. In these cases, choose a rating that is a goal, not just the next step up. Be optimistic and do not hold yourself back. When choosing your goal, be prepared to stretch yourself.

Rank

Next, deduct your 'Now' rating from your 'Goal' rating in each category to generate a priority ranking for each area. Circle the three highest ranking areas. If you find you have more than three categories running equal first, choose the three in which you feel the most confident in your strengths. Clearly, the higher the ranking, the more important it is to you to do something about it. These are areas where you have specific strengths yet you are underperforming. Often it is in your strongest areas where you are in need of the biggest stretch—usually because you are ignoring them by concentrating on areas where you are not as strong.

Action

You now come to 'Action'. Ironically, at this point you need to stop and rest. You have rated your performance and your situation. You have identified where you want to be, and you have acknowledged that you have strengths in all areas. You need to close your eyes, take three deep breaths and relax.

Imagine a dream in which you have reached your goal in one of your chosen areas. You wake up and it is achieved. It is an exciting and pleasing state to be in. What does it look like? What does it feel like? What is something you can look at, touch, smell or see? It may be a person, a thing, a process or anything imaginable. Think about the things you have done to get there. This is important. Work back slowly from that outcome to the very first step you took. What was it? That is the action you need to take today.

Don't overcomplicate this. It may be as straightforward as making a telephone call you have been putting off, or instructing someone to carry out a particular task, or booking a squash court, or buying some flowers.

Choose a simple action. Unless your goal is within very easy reach, you will not achieve it (or even come near it) today. What you want to do is take at least one step towards it. Write that step in the 'Action' column. You can have more than one step, but more than three is starting to build a project rather than taking an action. If it's a big task, break it down into small steps and use three of them.

Repeat this for two other areas. Go out of your way to make these actions immediately achievable. You should be able to do some of them in five minutes. At most they should take 15 minutes. It is important that they are simple steps. All they do is take you forward from where you are now. They get you moving.

At the end of this process, you will have a list of actions that you are capable of achieving in the three priority areas that will give the most leverage in improving your overall balance.

Do it now!

If you are in your workplace, do these things now. If you are somewhere where it is not possible to do this, open your diary and allocate the time when you will do it. There is probably nothing on your list that cannot be done now using your own resources, be they your personal assistant, your telephone, your email or yourself. If it means doing something face-to-face, go and see the person now. If you can't go now, make an appointment.

There is an immense amount of leverage to be gained by this very simple process. Throughout this book there will be calls to action—this is the first. The personal balance process is a simple way to make key things happen. Some people do this daily. Many do it monthly. It is especially useful if you feel stuck. Many of you may already do something like this regularly. If so, don't stop. If not, start now.

3 Recharge your management style
The management reboot

This could be the most productive day of your life. The 'management reboot' defrags your personal operating system. It eliminates backlogs of incomplete projects, clears away distractions in your workplace and initiates a habit of rational delegation. It helps you to manage people methodically.

How does it work?

Effective managers must have at least four basic skills if they are going to achieve anything:

1 They must be able to *focus* on the present. They have a lot to do and a limited amount of time. The more time they spend on non-essential activities, the less time they have to actually manage. They need to eliminate distraction.

2 They must be able to *delegate* effectively. Failure to do so means the right people won't be doing the right job. Plans fall behind. Targets are unmet. People don't develop and neither does the business. Ultimately that reflects on the manager. Failure to delegate can put a manager's job at risk.

3 They must be prepared to *act* when it is required. There are some things that only the managers can and must do. If they have focus and have delegated effectively, they will have time to apply their strengths and excel at what they do best.

4 They have to *prioritise*. Some things are best left till later. Some ideas, even some actions, need to be put aside until the time is right. It doesn't mean they are not important. They just aren't necessary right now.

Most managers have these skills; otherwise, they probably wouldn't be in their jobs. Yet many find their responsibilities overwhelming. I know I do. It is usually because I have let slip the four skills mentioned above. I have lost my focus; I'm trying to do everything; I'm too snowed under to take definitive action; and I can't work out what is important and what is not. It's time to reboot those skills.

What do I do? I clean my desk.

Sounds too simple? Probably; but not if you follow some hard and fast rules for putting those four skills to work.

To make this happen, focus on only one thing at a time. Pick up the first piece of paper on your desk. There are only four things you can do with it:

1   Nothing. It requires no focus. It has zero priority. It only distracts you. Eliminate that distraction now. Send it to the bin.
2   Something needs to be done by someone other than you. Delegate it now.
3   You have to do something, so take the *first* action to achieve that something now.
4   It doesn't have to be done now, so make a note of it and send it to the file. Whatever you do, move it off your desk. It is only a distraction.

Generate fast, efficient action

You have to apply these skills aggressively. You have to keep moving. Let's put them into simple terms that force action. For each document in your office (including all those magazines lying open at must-read pages), choose one of the following four imperatives.

1 Abandon it

So much of the stuff that piles up in a manager's office requires no action. It just sits around as a distraction. It builds up every month. Just bin it. If it's information, it's probably only an internet search away. It might have seemed like a good idea at the time, but the fact that it is hanging around means it is just not a priority. Get rid of it.

2 Manage it

Have someone do it. Who is the best person to handle that piece of paper? If it is not you, send it to that person. Ask them to take action. Managing people and resources is the core of your job. Move the paper off your desk and onto theirs.

3 Execute it

If it is something you have to do, do something *now*. Just don't try to do it all. Take the *first* step. Make the call, set up the meeting, or answer the email. If it is essential that you spend time on it, make an appointment with yourself—block out the time in your diary. In doing so, you end procrastination. You have already committed to the next step and you know when you are taking it.

4 Note it

If it is something that might be important in the future, make a note of it and send it to the relevant file.

Remember the acronym AMEN: abandon, manage, execute and note. Hardly rocket science, but extremely effective.

The results

Don't underestimate this simple process. If you have excessive clutter, it may take all day. However, it will be one of your most productive days. At the end of it you will have clarity. You will have achieved a huge amount of management in a short space of time. Your work space will be clear of distraction and you will be ready to move on and do what you are best at.

What you have done is apply the four basic management skills of focusing, delegating, acting and prioritising. If you have done this methodically, you will already have achieved four things. You will have:

1   cleared your work environment of distractions (so that you can focus on your job)
2   managed a number of issues and people in the most productive way possible (and so you now have more time to do your job)
3   taken the next step in executing some of your responsibilities (which is actually *doing* your job)
4   removed from your desk any nagging little things that you didn't know what to do with (that is, eliminated things that have no priority in your job).

There are a number of aids that can help you stay on track with this. Any time you want a reminder, go to the reboot workshop at <www.alanhargreaves.com> and download the short module called 'Set up a clear management platform'. It provides a series of short steps that keep you moving. To obtain details of a more thorough process, and an explanation of why it works, download the free e-book *The Management Reboot*.

This process produces even better results if you collaborate with someone else. They help you stick to the rules. But there is no reason why you cannot do it alone. Either start now, or block off time in your diary to do it. Just make sure that when that time comes, you don't do anything else until it is done.

4 Focus on your strengths

What are you really good at?

In chapter 3, you worked through a process to achieve mental and physical clarity in your work environment. You created a powerfully clear space so that you will have time to exert your best qualities. Those qualities are what will drive your management contribution. We need to identify what they are.

Clarity is a strong foundation. It's the platform on which you can truly manage your business and personal affairs—to everyone's benefit, including your own. Just as you need a clear space to work in, you need a clear view of how you work best in it.

In that space you have created, block off some time—an hour will do—in which you can focus on what you really bring to the management party. Like just about everything in this book, it will work better if you collaborate with someone else. You will still benefit if you do it on your own. However, other people can often see strengths in you that you can't see; or if you can see your strengths, you probably don't fully appreciate their value and power.

There are lots of ways to go about this. Employers and managers are increasingly aware that you benefit more from developing people's strengths than from improving their weaknesses. Academic research backs this up. And at the coalface, personal development experts such as Marcus Buckingham have written excellent, practical books on the topic. But we are not going to rush out and buy another book just yet. We want to act today. We will work with an available and well-understood model.

SWOT analysis

SWOT analysis meets both these criteria:

1 It is easily available. You can draw one up in about 20 seconds on any piece of paper.
2 It is well documented. Search for 'SWOT analysis' on the internet and you will find several million results.

SWOT stands for 'strengths, weaknesses, opportunities and threats'. It has been around for decades. It first appeared at Stanford University in the 1970s as a tool for developing corporate strategy. It has uses in that area, but also short-comings. They arise from expecting too much of what is basically an organising matrix. It may be misapplied, but it is also underappreciated, especially in management develop-ment. You may have used it when analysing a business issue, but you can generate real insight when you use it on yourself.

A SWOT matrix is simply a square with four quadrants, one for each of its component nouns, as shown in figure 4.1 (overleaf).

The objective of the analysis is to give direction to personal strategy. It focuses on areas that need attention and stimulates discussion about where opportunities lie. It does not generate a comprehensive plan, nor does it necessarily provide enough information to do so. But at the personal level it's an excellent starting point for assessing where and how you can make your best contribution for yourself, your team and your firm.

Why should you do this?

Because you are the manager. We made it clear in chapter 1 that you are going to make a big difference. Whatever you are charged with doing, you have to be dynamic. Yours is not a standstill job. You have to adapt to changing circumstances, you have to be creative and you have to act.

Figure 4.1: a SWOT matrix

Personal SWOT analysis	
Strengths:	Weaknesses:
Opportunities:	Threats:

Constantly. You will do all these things best in areas where you have strengths. Identifying your strengths will reveal opportunities to lead. Identifying weaknesses will provide opportunities to delegate and manage.

Do this process for three reasons:

1 to clarify how you will apply your strengths to your role
2 to find direction on what other roles are required for the ongoing management of the business
3 to see how the process works, because at some stage you are going to ask your immediate reports or individual team members to do the same process.

Complete the analysis

There are various versions of SWOT. Some differentiate between external forces (opportunities and threats) and internal ones (strengths and weaknesses). Others rearrange it into TOWS analysis — in other words, they do the process backwards. I don't know why.

We will keep it simple. Draw a square on a piece of paper and divide it into quadrants. (If you want a nice, clean published version with some instructions, go to <www.

alanhargreaves.com> and download one.) Throughout the process, stay open. Be honest. Think outside the square. Follow these guidelines:

❧ Read through the prompts in table 4.1 (overleaf) and use them to take a good look at yourself.

❧ Take your time. Try to spend a full hour on this. If you think you have finished, sit quietly for a few minutes. Other things will come up. Sleep on it if possible and review it the next day.

❧ Personal development works best when the person and the development are in the hands of different people. Ask colleagues—both senior and junior—for input; don't worry about appearing vulnerable. Most people will appreciate the work you are doing.

❧ Look for input from family and those who know you well; discuss the analysis with friends.

❧ Do not limit the number of items in each quadrant— brainstorm as many as possible.

❧ Look for connections between the quadrants.

❧ Remember that strengths suggest achievable opportunities.

❧ Weaknesses can be managed and threats can be acknowledged: by doing this, you can identify new opportunities.

❧ The process may raise a number of actions that you want to begin. Don't go overboard. Two or three are enough. Choose things that you can start right away and play to your strengths. List the rest for further investigation.

❧ The best actions will provide opportunities for you to use your strengths, manage your weaknesses and limit threats. They will be exciting for you and they will show you a clear way forward.

Table 4.1: SWOT analysis prompts

Strengths	Look for strengths that work for you. They are often indicated by things you are automatically good at, things you actually like doing, be they selling, filing, organising, writing, managing, communicating, supporting or promoting, just to name a few. You often do them better than others do. They can include: **Personal strengths:** loyalty, diligence, teamwork, ambition, commitment, analytical ability, creativity, honesty, sporting ability, studying skills, teaching skills **Skills:** technical ability, educational qualifications, courses completed, product knowledge, licences held, mathematical ability **Creativity:** the ability to develop new ideas in your area of responsibility, or the ability to put them into practice **Relationship strengths:** skills in relating to particular clients or sectors, suppliers, colleagues, management, family
Weaknesses	These are not your strong points. You often avoid them, or have someone else handle them. Some of them hinder your performance. They can include: **Poor administration skills:** disorganisation, laziness, lack of commitment, difficulty with certain types of people **Personal habits:** lateness, not looking after your health, untidiness, being short-tempered, lack of personal care **Lack of skills:** areas of performance that would improve with more training, functions you are simply unable to perform because you are not trained in them Essentially, this sector will contain the things you are not good at and should not be doing, or it will highlight the things you could do better if you had the right tools.
Opportunities	There are all sorts of opportunities to further your career or your business if you look for them. Many of these emerge from your strengths. If you look at what you are good at, you will discover ideas and projects that you

	are capable of developing. There is less effort—and more return for you—in seeking out opportunities that take your strengths from very good to excellent than there is in lifting your weaknesses from very poor to not bad. Look for ways to respond to changes in market conditions, your client profile, new product development, internal management structures and new technology, or simply design a project that you know will benefit you and the firm. Don't hesitate to propose it to management or your colleagues. Many great ideas are responses to threats, or ways of eliminating or delegating weaknesses.
Threats	Obstacles to your performance come from both inside and outside your career. They can include changing business conditions, personal issues, the people around you, the level of competition and changing technology, just to name a few. Basically this is a list of what could go wrong.
	Many threats can be countered by taking advantage of your strengths. But there are also those threats that suggest it will be best to structure your position so that you can avoid them or minimise their impact on you. Threats are a reality and need to be acknowledged. They will not simply disappear if you ignore them. Keep this in mind, but don't waste time on things you cannot control or change. Focus on the things you can control: your strengths and the opportunities they provide.

Move ahead

This analysis can have a powerful effect on your management. The way forward lies in the opportunity quadrant. You will have discovered in there some of the ideas that you have the vision and drive to see through to fruition.

The most powerful ones will be those that draw on your specific strengths. They will be projects or strategies that you actually want to do, that you can feel passionate about and that you can guide and motivate those around you to achieve. In many cases their implementation will address some of your weaknesses and minimise the risks apparent in the threats.

What you need to do now, however, is act. Focus on the three opportunities that, if acted upon, will have the strongest impact. Determine the steps required to take advantage of these opportunities. Keep these extremely simple. Break major tasks into small steps if you have to, but once you have identified them, give them momentum. Take the first step today.

Become the **expert** 5

Value your own ideas

We are all experts in something. Each one of us is better at something than most other people are. You see this in business all the time. I have been in board meetings where the most impressive result has been the quality of the minutes. Some people just have the knack of neatly summarising the entire process and clearly stating the outcomes. They should write books about how they achieve that. I can't do it, but I'd love to know how to. Right now, there are clients, customers and employees looking for advice in your area. Right now is the time to begin establishing yourself or your firm as the 'go to' source for information and advice on issues within your expertise.

The last four chapters have been concerned with clarifying roles and goals, and prompting action to develop management momentum. Now we will look at building management stature.

Identify and use your strengths

In difficult conditions, a common response is to do nothing. A mix of fear and risk avoidance can dominate decision making—within the firm and within the marketplace. What people need is advice they can trust and the comfort that someone has knowledge and expertise in the issues they are confronting. Yet, in these circumstances, we often find we are the ones looking for advice. We overlook the possibility that we could be the ones providing some. This is a natural position that many people assume: they believe that other people, not themselves, are the experts.

After working through chapter 4, you will have a far stronger view of where your natural expertise lies. Revisit that for a moment. The same process can be applied to businesses, or teams, or any group, to clearly identify their particular areas of expertise. What you need to do now is use that expertise in a way that publicly parades you, your team or your business.

Here are some examples of people and firms who have done this.

Saving by upgrading

A reseller of memory upgrades for laptops wrote a paper on what you should and should not consider when upgrading your memory. His key message was that it is cheaper to upgrade than it is to buy a new computer, and that an upgrade is just as effective. Great news in a recession. He had the local newspaper publish the paper in their small business section. As a result of this, he was able to launch a public-speaking career and now appears regularly at national conferences. This led to discussing the sale of his business to a national corporation.

The hair business

Libby Dedman opened her first hair salon when she was 21 years old. Later, when she had young children, she wanted to find a way for her business to continue without her being there all the time. She found that while she was interested in hairdressing, she had become more passionate about *managing* hair salons. Now she has three. Her most sought-after service today is not to do with hairstyles, but with running hairdressing businesses; she travels the world providing that advice. This grew from her participation at a national conference, where she spoke about how to set up a business like hers. That's what people wanted to know.

Useful advice

A legal firm had a surge of clients going through bankruptcy, wind-up, liquidation and damages claims. They held a highly publicised seminar on how to avoid these outcomes, and what to do if you can't. They promoted themselves as the 'go to' firm for legal risk management. Business improved accordingly. More importantly, the client base expanded so that when conditions improve, the firm will be able to offer other services to a greater number of customers.

Applying a hobby

A young staffer who is passionate about making home videos used his personal editing software to make a promotional DVD on how to apply one of the firm's services. None of the opposition was doing this. The sales team were ecstatic and asked for more. He made instructional videos across the product range. They were loaded onto the company website, which became the preferred source of product information in their sector. The staffer was promoted accordingly and eventually left to start his own business. His old firm now outsources to him.

A passion for food

Jessie Kirkness Parker, a trained chef, moved with her husband from South Africa to the Middle East in the 1970s. She found herself in a jurisdiction where women were not allowed to work without their father's or husband's consent — and women never worked as chefs! Yet she was passionate about the fusion of regional Arab cuisines in the Gulf region and retrained as a photojournalist with food in mind. The outlet for her energy was the first food column in the region, which her editor considered a waste of her good talent ('Writing about food is a waste of time!'). Times have changed and Jessie's first book, *A Taste of Arabia*, has gone on to win a prestigious Gourmand

World Cookbook Award in Paris. It has been designated the Best Arab Cookbook in the World, and Jessie advises the global hospitality industry on all matters related to cuisine, using her skills ranging from art direction to recipe creation.

Don't be afraid

Too many people avoid this sort of activity, often because of personal fears, shyness or false humility. Yet presenting your knowledge in a public forum can be a great source of personal development and can build your confidence immensely. If public speaking bothers you, it is probably a signal that you need to do a course in presentation skills. Don't hold back. You will find that a lot of people are in exactly the same position. If you are not sure about your written communication, work with an editor to analyse and improve your skills.

In short, don't let your own perspective hinder you from acknowledging your expertise. In his book *Outliers*, Malcolm Gladwell made the point that all of us end up as experts in something, often simply through the longevity of our experience. He suggests that about 10 000 hours is what it takes. That's about 10 years in any career, sport, hobby, pastime or other activity you are passionate about. My partner began coaching young horseriders as a hobby. She is now a sought-after instructor and publishes e-books on developing horseriding skills.

Simple steps you can take now

Begin developing your expertise now:

1 *Brainstorm*. Think about your own possibilities on the basis of the strengths in your own organisation, or those that you have yourself. You can be the 'go to' person in your own firm, and your firm can be the 'go to' firm in your industry.

2   *Start small.* This is not an expensive exercise. Approach the local Rotary Club or Chamber of Commerce and propose a presentation on something that you or your firm knows about. You will be surprised at the response. Community groups are always looking for new ideas and speakers.

3   *Reuse it.* Use the event to develop a prototype presentation that you can call up at any time. Turn it into a video and put it on the web.

4   *Work with your local newspaper or an industry magazine.* Turn your presentation into an article and have it published. The easiest way to do this is to record your presentation, then write it up and edit it into a publishable article.

5   *Be available.* Offer yourself as a spokesperson to journalists who cover your sector.

6   *Hold a seminar.* Choose a theme that focuses on the information that people use to make decisions about your product and your industry. If you cannot cover the entire program with your own expertise, invite keynote speakers, or examine whether collaborating with some of your customers or suppliers will make a more compelling conference. They will appreciate the opportunity. Invite your local newspaper or representatives of the media that cover your industry. Video some of the speakers and put excerpts on your website. Develop your site as a centre for information and excellence.

This is a great way to bring in business, boost your stature and lift your career at virtually no cost. It focuses on your strengths and works particularly well in tough times. The beauty of it is that when the cycle turns, you have already established yourself as the best qualified person who was there in difficult times, not just when things were going well.

Start your own think tank

The power of several

Once a month I have dinner with four friends. We are an odd mix, and there is a 20-year span between the oldest and the youngest in the group. We have one thing in common: we are all interested in business and ideas.

Mostly we just shoot the breeze. But we always finish with one simple process. It has four steps and it doesn't take long:

1 First, we go around the table and each describe something that went right in the last week.
2 Next, we go around and describe something that went wrong.
3 Then we each run through something we want to get right in the coming week.
4 As the last step, we each describe how we imagine each other getting that thing right.

The results are astounding. I have never left without a new idea or a new perspective. It might be something out of left field, something I just haven't thought of. Or it might be something I already know but I am just not doing. Suddenly my options open up; my thinking is refreshed; I move onto a positive track. The following week is always more productive.

Why does it work?

No-one has a monopoly on the best ideas. Whenever you work through a proposal with a group of people, you will always arrive at an outcome that is better than your original. This doesn't diminish your role—it enhances it.

Managing in isolation is a dangerous practice. You limit yourself and your options. It is worse when times are difficult and you believe that the current situation is all due to you. You might rightfully accept responsibility for the state of things, but you wrongfully blame yourself for it. You can cut off interaction with others and close your vision to new opportunities. Then the way out is shut.

Break out of this rut simply by asking for help. It's the easiest and most efficient way to turn things around.

A think tank, however, offers much more than that. It is an opportunity to dramatically broaden your range of possibilities. With a diverse mix of people, you can explore ideas you might never have thought of. It gives you a creative platform—one that keeps you at the leading edge of your industry. You don't have to be in a rut to benefit from one. With a well-structured think tank, you can take a perfectly functioning business and lift it to an even higher level. That should be the goal of every business. That is where you want to be.

What can you do?

Think tanks can be informal get-togethers, or more structured, scheduled meetings. Some are business-based; others are lifestyle-based; some are heavily skewed towards mentoring. The essential ingredient is that the members are different enough in their thinking (or their chosen paths) for their insights to be outside the boundaries of your own thinking.

How do you set up a think tank?

The difference between a think tank and a dinner party is structure. There must be a topic and a process for thinking about it. To develop a think tank, you need three things:

1 people who want to participate
2 a topic to focus on
3 tools to address the issues.

Start this with a small group. Don't try to force people into it. You want people who are eager to contribute. It's a two-way street. You might suggest the first topic, saying you need help on it. But make it clear that any member can raise any issue they want to explore at future sessions.

Exactly who should be in the group will depend on what you want to achieve. It can be a loose arrangement like a monthly dinner, or something more specific. A recovery think tank might want a panel of participants who meet regularly to assess the latest industry data or market intelligence. This is not a board or a management committee. It is a think tank charged with assessing your chances of spotting recovery and of taking advantage of it. It works best if you include views from outside your business or industry. That sparks ideas and identifies opportunities. If you are a one-person business, ask friends and other business acquaintances to swim in your tank. If you are part of a larger corporation, draw on people in diverse departments. Attract people who think differently from you, and if you are lucky, differently from everyone else. So choose your team creatively.

Make it clear what you want to achieve. Use an agenda for every meeting. Always have a specific topic, but let the discussion go wherever it leads. That is where the creativity lies.

If you are struggling with a decision, your think tank is the place to take it. It will provide you not only with the input to make hard decisions, but also with the support to put them in place with confidence.

Tools you can use

Look for stimulating input. Invite a guest speaker to talk about something you don't usually think about. Try using chapters of this book. Circulate one to members and discuss the issues it raises.

Use the established toolkit of management techniques. Here are a few simple, tried and tested suggestions:

꘎ *Brainstorm future scenarios.* Start with a 'what if' and work through the impact. What would a shift in the business environment mean for your staff, your product, your market or your industry? If suddenly everyone could access everything on high-speed broadband, what would happen to you? Where would it take you? Do you want to go there? What would you have to do to get there?

꘎ *Analyse the risks involved in any new strategy.* Forecasting business performance is high risk. It is rare for a new strategy to perform exactly in line with expectations. Forecasts are usually either too optimistic or too pessimistic. A think tank broadens the range of opinions. Rather than being too positive or too negative, a think tank might just come up with a more realistic plan.

꘎ *Don't avoid some of the popular or often-used techniques.* Even if you have done them before, they can still be useful. Just apply them to a new issue. Explore techniques like PEST analysis, SWOT analysis, product mix analysis, appreciative enquiry and open space technology. They all add value to the way you review any issue and can help you use your think tank to expand your management thinking.

Anytime is a good time to experiment with business thinking, but now is always best. This makes sense in any enterprise, large or small. I have seen participation in think tanks turn into one of the most productive and motivating management practices.

7 Surf the cycle

The business cycle is not dead

Bob Ansett started Budget Rent A Car in 1965. Over the next decade he built up a formidable enterprise. Then, when the 1974 recession started to bite, Budget hit the wall. Business spending decreased, flowthrough from airports collapsed and car rentals slumped. Budget needed customers and cash flow.

Until that time, if you rented a car in Australia, the odometer was checked on your return and you were charged according to the distance travelled. That year Ansett changed the system. Customers who paid in advance were charged a competitive flat rate regardless of distance travelled. This strategy achieved two things:

1   It brought in more customers.
2   It brought in cash more quickly.

It also helped clients easily estimate the cost of a business trip.

Ansett's response to the recession changed the car rental payment system forever. Times were still tough, but when the recession lifted, Budget emerged with a significantly higher market share, which laid the groundwork for even greater success. For Ansett and Budget, recession turned out to be an opportunity.

The sun also rises

Imagine you are in the middle of a recession. The economic conditions in your industry have not turned around. They may be getting worse. You don't know how long they will continue to deteriorate. And you certainly don't know when they'll improve. What is the only thing you can be certain of?

What does history tell us? Since 1948, there have been 10 recessions in the US. That's so far. The figure is roughly the same for most Western economies, including Australia, although recently it has performed better than most. Still, there have been five technical recessions in Australia since the 1960 credit squeeze, and if you add a couple of significant downturns, the number of tough times increases to seven. What does that tell us about recessions?

↦ There are lots of them.
↦ They last for different periods of time.
↦ They don't last forever.

It is also clear that there is one about every six to eight years. According to actuarial studies, the average life span is currently around 80 years. In other words, if you are 40 today, it is likely that you will live through at least another five recessions. It may be a cliché to say that life is not a dress rehearsal, but recessions are. The only thing you can be certain about is that although the economy recedes, it also recovers.

What you need to know

It is essential that you acknowledge this fact. Stay positive. It is important that you don't stick your head in the sand when the going gets tough. But it is also important to remember that there is a cycle. Don't just think about the seven recessions; remember the seven recoveries. In difficult times, you, your firm and your employees need to maintain confidence that you are survivors, and that you are going to harvest greater rewards in the recovery phase of the business cycle. For many firms, relative success depends on how well you surf this wave.

Business downturns are not always national. They can occur just in your sector. Those conditions might be telling you something. If you are facing hard times, is it time for some bold action? It could be an opportunity to do one or more of the following:

➪ *Rethink your business.* Recessions highlight marginal activities. They don't just weed out the weaker competitors—they spotlight your weakest operations. Are you hanging on to business lines that simply don't make the cut?

➪ *Make hard decisions.* Clearing away the asset clutter of unsustainable operations can raise cash, cut maintenance and free resources for activities with better prospects.

➪ *Differentiate your product or service.* Ansett's strategy boosted both cash flow and market share. Can you step outside the square and experiment with new ideas?

➪ *Buy new business lines, merge or form strategic alliances.* Everyone is under pressure. Collaboration may be the path to survival and prosperity.

➪ *Reassert timeless principles.* Receivables management can become sloppy in good times. When was the last time you reviewed your credit policy? Is it time to tighten your systems across the board?

➪ *Start planning for recovery.* Sometimes improvements come sooner than you expect. Will you be ready?

To put your cyclical thinking on track, turn on your economic radar. Become increasingly aware of subtle shifts in the environment and the possibilities they may represent. Start now by developing your own set of leading indicators.

Where to look

We all tend to focus on the national indicators. These are the ones that are sensationalised by the media. Apart from the fact that they are usually negative and depressing, the real problem with these is that they are seldom identified as either *leading* or *lagging* indicators. They are usually generalised numbers chosen for their news value, not for their relevance to current conditions, let alone conditions in your particular sector.

For example, unemployment is widely recognised as a lagging indicator. Unemployment is often at its worst well after other indicators have turned positive and the economy is starting to move ahead. It reflects the tendency of management to be slow in laying people off and equally slow in bringing them back on. Hiring (or firing) staff is a bigger decision than simply restocking (or destocking) inventory. It is therefore not one that is taken lightly.

Leading indicators include items such as the direction of the stock market, the number of new jobless claims being made, new home approvals and credit conditions. You need to be familiar with these, but for your own situation you need to be acutely aware of conditions in your own industry. For example:

- What is happening to your input prices? If they are rising, has inventory run-down reached the bottom? Conversely, have the prices reached a level that suggests a bubble is developing?
- Is there plenty of suitable labour available or are there signs that some competitors are hiring? Are resources being shifted into or out of your sector?

Understand credit markets

Possibly the clearest signals come from changing conditions in financial markets. Just as your own credit rating indicates how much money you can personally borrow, the terms on which banks are lending to business is a key indicator of economic conditions. Don't concentrate on the rate. The important elements are the margin that banks are charging over their cost of money and their preparedness to lend.

Banks basically cover their risk in three ways:

1 They demand security.
2 They limit the amount they will let you borrow.
3 They charge an interest rate based on their assessment of the risk of lending to you.

We will return to the first two in more detail in a later chapter. But for now, just concentrate on the interest rate.

This is easy to monitor. The cash rate is set by the Reserve Bank of Australia (RBA). At the time of writing, it was relatively low at 4.75 per cent, but it has been as high as 14 per cent in the last 20 years. In theory, it goes down when conditions decline and starts rising as conditions improve. It is not surprising that the rate was close to all-time lows in 2009, or that it started to rise as recovery set in towards the end of that decade. The rise didn't mean that banks would suddenly lend large amounts of money. It just meant that the RBA analysis suggested things were improving.

The rate you have to pay is obviously a lot higher than the cash rate. The extent to which it is higher is the 'margin'. When the cash rate was 3 per cent, the overdraft rate was about 8.25 per cent, a margin of 5.25 per cent. That's relatively high. In the middle of the 2000s, when conditions were relatively buoyant, the cash rate was often around 5 per cent, but the overdraft rate was about 8 per cent, giving a margin of only 3 per cent.

The margin is a fair indicator of business conditions and it is easy to monitor. All banks publish their rates in the business press each week. What is the margin for your industry? Call your banker and ask. You don't have to apply for a loan to find out the information, and you will develop a feel for what is happening. If it is becoming easier for you to borrow money, it is becoming easier for everyone else, including your customers and suppliers.

Start your own business indicators

To keep yourself financially aware, set up a short list of simple economic indicators that you can easily monitor. Some ways you could do this are:

✇ *Put in place systems of gaining market intelligence.* Develop relationships with suppliers to keep track of what is really happening out there. Maintain a dialogue with your bankers.

✇ *Focus on your industry.* Look less at national numbers and more at what is happening to the people who make and buy your product.

Management needs to know both the big picture and the one that is relevant to you. Setting up your own business indicators is a simple way of keeping your radar scanning the business environment at both the macro and micro levels. These indicators keep you alert to downturns, which can call for hard decisions. But remember that downturns can also present new opportunities—be open to them.

8 Address uncomfortable issues

How to handle difficult situations

Few of us will go through our careers without having to face issues we don't want to. These issues may involve things that we don't have the confidence or skills to handle well, or they may involve situations we find uncomfortable or even threatening. Often we simply don't handle them at all. We hope they will just go away, or sort themselves out. They usually don't, and they often become worse if left alone.

The first rule in handling these situations is this: don't manage them alone.

Leadership can be a lonely task, but it should not be practised in isolation. Functional leaders regularly refer to others—partners, boards, chairpersons, directors, mentors, consultants, friends and colleagues—about difficulties they are facing. They do this because they know, consciously or unconsciously, that their own thoughts may cloud their judgement, lead them in the wrong direction, or curb their ability to act. Consider just two personal feelings that we are all capable of:

1   *Fear.* Nobody likes to talk about it, but we all have it.
    It is one of the most powerful instincts. It saves us from
    death and injury. It helps us avoid all sorts of danger.
    It warns us of consequences. It can help us do the right
    thing. It is central to our survival. But if it is suppressed
    rather than acknowledged, it can run wild. It needs
    to be kept in perspective. Unacknowledged, fear can
    lead to wrong action, inaction, procrastination or
    'analysis paralysis'.

2   *Anger.* This is equally powerful, but often harder to acknowledge because we so often feel justified in our anger. And maybe we are. But it does not lead to solutions with any longevity. Too often, it produces a bandaid for the problem or a short-lived but destructive 'letting off of steam' and, later on, more of the same. The result is often just high levels of staff turnover.

The problem with these instinctive responses is that they are part of our makeup, and so they are difficult to manage. Our perspective is like a hall of mirrors. Alone, our chances of objectivity are limited, and therefore so are our choices. Often it looks like we have none. So, our plan for addressing uncomfortable issues starts with talking to someone else.

How to approach the situation

Read through the following hypothetical but common business situation. It could generate fear, anger, stress and financial trouble. We will refer to this example later in the chapter.

You are the general manager of a medium-sized manufacturing business in a reasonably competitive sector. Your largest customer, Louise, is consistently late in payment, to the extent that it is now causing cash flow difficulties. You have found her to be aggressive and difficult to deal with. Also, you do not get on particularly well with Joshua, the salesperson who handles this account. You are concerned that he will leave, or work against you. He has the loyalty of the sales team. This is all too hard. As a result, you have not addressed the situation with Louise, Joshua or the sales team. This procrastination has only made the situation worse. What do you do?

Step 1: Get advice

You may already have a mentor or friend whom you bounce things off. If not, you need to find one. It may be someone inside or outside your firm. The key thing is that you can be honest with them. It may be someone with no understanding of your business whatsoever—this is often where the most refreshing perspectives come from. It may be more than one person. But once you have set up a meeting with them, prepare your thoughts on the remaining steps and walk through the process with them.

Step 2: Define your preferred outcome

Define exactly the result that you want. Whatever the issue is that you are concerned about, imagine exactly what outcome would be the perfect result—the result that would make you feel you have fully addressed the problem and it has been solved. Review this solution with your mentor. It will put some objective reality around your goal.

For our example, the stress-free future might look something like this: Louise remains a key client and adheres to mutually agreed payment terms; you are able to plan accordingly; your sales relationship with Louise remains strong; your customer base broadens; your cash flow is positive; your sales team is pleased with the result (and so are you).

Step 3: Acknowledge your concerns

Clearly state your emotional responses to the issues involved in reaching your goal. Is the task before you too daunting? Do you think you will fail? Does it require confrontations you don't want to have? Do you feel underskilled? Do the people involved scare you? Are you worried people will leave? Is your primary concern what the impact will be on you and your reputation or status?

Make a list of issues or people that trigger these responses, then write down your honest feelings in regard to each one. For example, are you scared of confronting a particular person, or you are fearful of professional failure? You don't have to show this list to anyone, but you need to be able to honestly articulate your feelings when you discuss them with your adviser. Acknowledging these reactions is the first step towards getting them into perspective. They will be clearer still when you have openly discussed them with someone else.

Step 4: Introduce objectivity

For each of the responses in step 3, write down an objective assessment of the issue or person. Compare this objective reality with your subjective concerns. For example:

↣ Louise:

- Concerns: she is scary; you don't want to confront her; you fear losing the account.
- Reality: she also runs a commercial business; she uses your product for a reason; she manages a tight ship; she may be under pressure you can't see.

↣ Joshua:

- Concerns: you don't feel he will back you in finding a remedy.
- Reality: he is your employee; he has a job to do and targets to meet; you have a responsibility to support him, but you also have a responsibility to manage the interests of the whole firm, not just the sales team.

↣ Failure:

- Concerns: your actions will fail and you will look weak.
- Reality: this is a commercial issue; you have a responsibility to manage it; the real failure is the failure to address it; doing nothing will make you look weak.

Once you have made objective evaluations that are separate from your emotional responses, you can be satisfied that you have acknowledged your concerns but have put them in perspective. Then you can focus on the realities.

Step 5: Improve your hand

Look again at the realities that you outlined in step 4. What is the most appropriate attitude to take to them? The answer is straightforward: be businesslike. One of the key advantages of the business model is that it is based on commercial principles. The goal is not usually fluffy. The measures of success are clear to all. Do not feel restrained by petty politics. Stick to the facts. The facts are exactly what you outlined under 'Reality' in step 4. So what do you do?

In our example, you are going to have to approach Louise. Not with emotions, just with the facts. You will make it clear that there is a problem and that you are looking for a solution that is good for both parties. The solution will have lasting power if it benefits both of you, so think through the following before you approach her. You need to strengthen your hand, but in a way that is attractive to her. Let your sales team know this is an issue that has to be managed. Ask for their suggestions on a solution and consider the following:

⋙ Can you make your product more appealing to Louise?
⋙ If you find she is under pressure, what can you do to help?
⋙ Do you have rigorous payment terms that are unrealistic?
⋙ Do the payment terms accommodate key customers?
⋙ Is Louise already receiving preferred terms? Does she know this?
⋙ What services, discounts or payment plans can you offer that would encourage prompt payment?
⋙ Can you offer better delivery or better value for money?
⋙ What is your bottom line here? What terms can you afford?

None of these should detract from the central issue of addressing your payment problem. Nonetheless, considering them will strengthen your perspective and prepare you for whatever direction the conversation takes.

Step 6: Take action

It is important that you personally take the lead on this issue. There are very important reasons for this. Take our example. By deferring the matter to your sales team, you have diminished your leadership power. It has shifted from you to those above you and below you—the customer and the sales team. By postponing action, you have let the situation fester. Your own stress levels have risen as a result. That, in turn, is affecting your actions, or bringing about inaction.

By taking the lead on this, you will make it clear that this is a real issue for the firm. Your action of speaking to the customer will give the issue much more credibility. The customer will more sincerely believe that the business relationship is an important one and that you want to do your utmost to ensure its integrity. It will also be clear to your sales team that the business relationship is between two firms, not just between the customer and the sales team.

This action is not magic, but it has been my experience that most people respond positively to such an approach. Even 'difficult' people. It becomes clear that your business is managed on a commercial basis, that you don't shirk issues, that you look for solutions, and that you value relationships. In the example we have used, you have reasserted the relationship with the firm rather than with the salesperson. You will be in a stronger position to manage the situation should he depart.

Step 7: Review

Review this process honestly with your third party. What has worked? What hasn't? Other issues arise in each of these steps. In our example, there might be items such as whether the sales team appraisal/incentives should include income recovery targets, whether you should launch a mission to broaden your customer base, whether you are concerned about team loyalty, and if so what you could do about it.

The results

Much is written about leadership in business. Most of us have misgivings about our adequacies in some areas. The process outlined here has helped me through numerous situations where I have found myself procrastinating. One of the best ways to develop leadership qualities, boost your confidence and develop respect among your colleagues is to methodically address uncomfortable issues.

Identify your strongest assets
Simplify your business

'Keep it simple.' It's a slogan that gets a lot of air time these days. In some situations it just helps you calm down; in others it reminds you that things don't have to be that hard. In business it can lead to the most effective strategies. Keeping it simple prompts both action and results. There should be no surprises about this. The simpler something is, the easier it is to achieve. The easier it is to achieve, the more likely it is to be done. So why do we make things so complicated and what can we do about it?

There is nothing new here. The same goes for a lot of sensible business thinking. Look at the number of people who find inspiration in the writings of the ancient Chinese general Sun Tzu. Reading of his *Art of War* reminds us that not much has changed. We just forgot some basics along the way.

Keeping it simple also has old roots.

Meet William of Ockham. This 14th-century English logician is credited with inventing what is known as 'Ockham's razor'. Essentially it means that the correct explanation for just about anything is usually the simplest one. (It is likely that William never actually used the term 'razor'; his name is associated with the philosophical principle called the 'law of parsimony', which supports the reduction of explanations to their simplest correct form.) By taking this razor to complicated scenarios and cutting away unnecessary assumptions and data, you arrive at the most likely explanation for the way things are. In general, complicated explanations prove to be wrong more often than simple ones do.

Simplicity and business

In modern business, we do not need to look far to find the advantages of applying Ockham's thinking. For example, the best websites are the ones that are easiest to navigate. If the message is clear and the result is one click away, the customer will probably click on it. If two clicks are needed, you start to lose customers. It's downhill from there. According to one study, 83 per cent of the people who search on Google do not search beyond the first page of results. The fact is we are generally time-poor and overwhelmed with information, maybe even spoilt by it. This puts a premium on convenience. In this environment, convenience means fewer decisions.

Now for 'convenience', read 'simplicity'. The 'elevator speech' can have as much impact as a 30-minute presentation. On YouTube, the most-watched videos peak at 57 seconds. Why is Google the dominant search engine? There are probably several reasons, but one is the design of the home page. There is virtually nothing on it. No tower ads. No involuntarily loaded commercials. Just 'Google', in big letters, and a big box to type in what you are searching for. Originally, the more crowded home pages of many competitors just didn't offer that simplicity. Eventually they did, but by then Google had stolen the show.

The most popular products are invariably the ones that solve the customer's problem with a minimum of fuss and for which they have to make the fewest decisions. And this applies in all facets of business. The simplest solution is often the best: it is easier to understand; it is quicker to implement; and fewer things can go wrong with it.

Even the share prices of companies with messy structures generally trade at a discount to simpler ones. In the global financial crisis (GFC), firms with heavily engineered financial structures suffered more than others. The focus of most supply-chain projects is how to simplify them. Joint managing directorships often fail. One seems to be better. When you are asked to join the loyalty program at the checkout, do you have time to fill out the form? Can you be bothered? When asked to register on a new website, do you falter when you see the amount of information required? Are you more likely to register on one that asks for no more than your email address?

Simplicity can be key to fulfilling the mission. In reviewing any part of your business, ask what you can do to make it simpler.

Simplicity and management

Ask also what you can do to make your management task simpler. In chapter 4, we looked at identifying your own strengths. The SWOT process helps many people see that they spend far too much time on things they are not good at. This brings us to another historical figure who has had a significant impact on modern business thinking.

Vilfredo Pareto was an Italian economist. At the beginning of the 20th century, he noted that the distribution of wealth, at least at that time in Italy, was roughly in the proportion 80:20. That is, about 80 per cent of wealth, certainly in the form of land at least, was held by about 20 per cent of the people. He went on to note that this ratio seemed to apply to all sorts of situations, and so the 80:20 rule was born.

Just as we are not sure whether William of Ockham ever talked of razors, it is not clear whether Pareto talked of 80:20. But, over time, he has been credited with the thinking behind the term. Many have elaborated on it since. When we look around us, it is not hard to see the evidence for its existence.

In terms of your management strengths, it is very much the case. The activities you undertake that really make a difference to the business are often confined to a limited amount of your available time. As we pointed out earlier, there are good reasons for this, the main one being that people end up spending more time on things they are not good at because, obviously, they are not efficient at these tasks. The 80:20 rule can help you focus efforts on what is really making a difference. What is your most productive 20 per cent?

Using 80:20

Take the issue of customer relations. If you monitor the various causes of customer dissatisfaction, a pattern will often emerge. For example, there may be far more people irked by waiting time in a coffee shop than there are people annoyed by the price. Maybe the fewest complaints are about the quality of the coffee, or the tidiness of the premises or the friendliness of the staff.

If the goal is to boost customer loyalty, the 80:20 rule shows you where to apply Ockham's razor. In the coffee shop example, we listed five sources of customer complaint (waiting time, price, quality, tidiness and friendliness). A thorough survey may well find that 80 per cent of the irritation comes from only one source. Remember that one source is only 20 per cent of the total number of sources; that is, one out of five. Rather than being overwhelmed by the thought of completely reinventing your customer service policy, your first, simple task is to address the main source. That will probably reduce your complaints by 80 per cent. This is one reason why this book does not always shy away from so-called bandaid solutions. Sometimes the simplest change you can implement can have the quickest and strongest impact.

Pareto and Ockham work well together. Quality management systems are often based on them. In a list of the most common causes of product failure, the main culprit often fits the 80:20 ratio or a ratio close to it. Once that fault is fixed, quality assurance surges, because 80 per cent of failures have been eliminated. And, once that one is fixed, a second application of the rule will isolate the next 80 per cent of the now-reduced number of product failures. It keeps the process simple, actionable and successful.

Take a simple approach

Having a keen eye on the real drivers of your business is central to effective management. Look at your own business—what can you identify as your strongest suits? For example:

⇨ Which products produce most of your revenue or, even more importantly, most of your profit margin?

⇨ Which 20 per cent of your management skills create 80 per cent of your input into your business success?

⇨ Which marketing teams generate most of the sales?

⇨ Which promotional activities achieve the best results?

Can you take clear and immediate action here? Can you enhance the already-strong performance of those efforts by investing more in them rather than applying resources elsewhere?

Take care

This leads us to our last point: take care of your best people.

Who are they? Around 20 per cent of them are probably responsible for 80 per cent of your success. Maybe they won't be getting big bonuses this year, but make it clear that they are special. Invite them to your think tank or keep them close to you and your decision making. If they are that good, they will be sought by the opposition. Show that they are key players on your team and that together you are planning to come out of this front and centre. If you have a budget for special remuneration, focus it on them. They are the key drivers of your team.

Be open

Innovation and business

Too often, we ascribe the notion of creativity to only the obvious avenues—art, writing, acting and so on. The truth is, addressing a business issue requires creative thinking. Maintaining a narrow view can keep us trapped in the problem, but creative thinking frees us to find a solution. The hard part is working out how to do this.

In *What Made You Think of That?*, Gary Bertwistle's guide to thinking differently in business, there is a fascinating appendix outlining what the author learned from working with rock bands. Apart from relating interesting anecdotes, this appendix shows how creative ideas can emerge from all areas of life experience. We only need to look.

In order to see, though, we need to be open.

Why *not* knowing everything can help

Take this simple example from my own experience.

I am not a great believer in astrology. I don't dismiss it out of hand, but I can't really see the connection between the stars and my life.

However, I do have some thoughts that keep me agnostic on the idea. I am aware that the position of the moon can shift entire oceans. So at a stretch, I might accept the possibility that the forces of the universe may have an effect on life on Earth—even to the point that they may have had a subtle tidal impact on, say, my foetal blood pressure.

From there, I can also allow that, at the moment of my birth, when I took my first breath, the flow of blood to my brain was therefore such that certain neurons were turned on in my brain before others. That, in turn, gave me certain behavioural characteristics that may reflect the configuration of the constellations relative to Earth at that time.

I do not know if this is true. But I do know that there is a lot we don't know. To be quite honest, my own thinking tells me the world is flat, even though I am regularly told this is not the case. And I will never understand gravity.

So, as an astrological agnostic, I don't go out of my way to read my horoscopes. I do, however, read them in the dentist's waiting room, or in one of my daughter's fashion magazines lying around the family room, and during idle time, when I have nothing to do. This probably happens once a year, so let's say I've read about 50 of them.

In 1982, I was a freelance business journalist in Hong Kong with one small child, one on the way and very little money coming in. I was sitting in the kitchen reading the *South China Morning Post*, wondering what to do about this, when I casually read the Piscean horoscope for that week. It suggested that now was a good time to embrace change and that I should seek a different 'medium' to apply my 'interests' to.

This wasn't a burning bush moment. I did not experience white light. But it did trigger something in me. From 'medium', I got the word 'media'. That gave me television. My 'interest' was business. Maybe other people would be interested in business television.

I spent the rest of the day putting together a proposal for a business television program. I contacted a commercial broadcasting network the next week and put it to them. They loved it, but they weren't going to do it because it was in English. Their priority was to boost ratings for their Chinese channels, which was something I couldn't help them with. I put the idea to one side.

Three months later, I had lunch with a friend who brought along the Director of Broadcasting for RTHK, Hong Kong's equivalent of the ABC. I mentioned the idea in passing. It turned out that RTHK were looking to do something in that space. He loved the idea. I did a screen test the next week and three months later I was the Financial Editor of RTHK.

As it turned out, the program never went to air on television. Instead, it became a radio program. Also, I was able to anchor the financial piece on a current affairs program. This was not a bad result, and it gave me a high profile in pro-business Hong Kong. Two years later, and just prior to the birth of my third child, I was headhunted by a stockbroking firm. Three years later I was a director of that firm and well into a 20-year career that I found incredibly rewarding, for both myself and my growing family.

Give all thoughts a chance

The first rule of brainstorming is to reject no idea. I am not saying that my life is a result of how the constellations were situated at the time of my birth. Maybe it was; maybe it wasn't. Nor was reading that horoscope in my kitchen the only prompt that made everything happen. But I can say that when I read it, I was open to any interpretation that could be put on it.

Out of my estimated 50 readings, something has been prompted on only two or three occasions, so I am not suggesting basing a life strategy on it. The key point is that there are opportunities to think outside the square all around us. We only need to stay open for when they are passing by.

Try a simple exercise

Dean Collier is one of Australia's leading experts in putting you in touch with the source of your intuition. He uses all sorts of techniques to help people focus on their uniqueness, often with remarkable results.

One such technique uses numbers. Now before you say, 'Here we go again', let me say that my view on numerology is pretty much the same as it is on astrology. However, I have tried some of Collier's techniques and they have provided me with some quite exciting opportunities for lateral thinking regardless of the depth of my belief in the theory. Stay open while we draw on some of his ideas.

Through his work on the frame of humanity, Collier has used various techniques to distill our unique, yet predictable, patterns of influence and has related them to the numerology of our birth. In table 10.1, by day of birth, there are 27 characteristics associated with his key nine human essences. For example, a person born on the 5th, 14th or 23rd day of the month would be associated with the characteristics freedom, communication and knowledge.

Table 10.1: Collier's characteristics linked to birth date

Day of birth	Characteristics
1, 10, 19, 28	Individual, will, compromise
2, 11, 20, 29	Cooperation, diplomacy, confidence
3, 12, 21, 30	Self-expression, challenges, logical
4, 13, 22, 31	Discipline, change, opposites
5, 14, 23	Freedom, communication, knowledge
6, 15, 24	Responsibility, care, unity
7, 16, 25	Wisdom, thoughts, trends
8, 17, 26	Authority, ambitions, limitations
9, 18, 27	Compassion, family, specialise

Now try this:

1 Write down a particular issue or plan that you are working on. It can be anything at all, small or large, really important or relatively not so. There is probably something that is going on in your personal or business life right now

that will come to mind. If you are struggling to think of something, go back to the lists we developed in earlier chapters or revisit those processes to prompt ideas.

2   Locate your day-born number and identify the key characteristics associated with it. Write these down on a piece of paper.

3   Take a moment to think about what those words mean for you. Don't focus on whether you can relate them to your personal traits. Simply reflect on what positive thoughts they evoke.

4   Now reflect on your own history and see if you can recognise any point, event or process in your business or personal life where one of those characteristics has formed part of a positive experience.

5   Think openly about how your application of that characteristic, or your participation in it, or simply your presence, contributed to the result.

6   Now take those thoughts and imagine how you might apply that same characteristic to your current situation.

For me, this process can suggest different ways of going about things. It has often thrown up a 'next best step' and it has laid the groundwork for choosing a future direction.

Be open to ideas

There is more to be said about Collier's nine human essences. All of them contain words with great evocative power. I know of people who have used words outside of their birth dates to generate creative thinking. You may think that this defeats the purpose. It does if you follow numerology, but it doesn't if you are looking to think outside the square.

Leverage this process with a partner. Relate to each other the example of where the characteristic played a part in your lives. Then, rather than applying it to your current situation, ask them how they would apply it.

The point of this exercise is not so much the application of your birth characteristics to your life strategy, even if there is something to be said for that. Rather, it is to reinforce the view that we are surrounded by tools to prompt creative solutions. Clinging to closed beliefs puts limitations in place. Being open to the universe removes them. An effective manager cannot afford to have a closed mind.

PART II

Recharge your finances

Managers often give finance a wide berth. They know they shouldn't, but finance and accounting rarely inspire them. Yet finance can be interesting, and it can be simple. No financial theory is impenetrable. In this section, you will explore financial concepts in a way that can change how you think about your business. You will learn what working capital management actually means. You will understand the valuation techniques of investment bankers. You will feel confident making decisions about owning, leasing, buying and selling. You will manage your money better and you will know how to develop a workable policy to collect what is owed to you.

Review the essentials

Why cash flow is more important than profit

Cash flow is the key to business success in good times. In bad times, it is the essence of survival. A lack of cash kills businesses. They don't go bankrupt if they fail to make a profit; they go bankrupt when they don't have any money.

How insufficient cash makes businesses fail

Consider the following example. You've set up Prosthomed.com, a web-based business that collects and collates information on prosthetics. Your target market is the medical profession. Prosthomed.com generates advertising income and earns commission on products purchased via the site. You have built a powerful, interactive website, employed three people, marketed the site and sold advertising on it. Your initial forecasts of how much will be spent setting up and managing Prosthomed.com in the first year are shown in table 11.1.

Table 11.1: forecast costs for Prosthomed.com

Item	Amount ($)
Marketing and advertising	30 000
Rent	16 000
Website development	50 000
Wages and salaries	120 000
Website support	15 000

This expenditure will be spread over the 12 months, subject to the needs of the business. Based on your expected timing of these expenses, you forecast the cash outflows to be as shown in table 11.2. They rise from $59000 in the first quarter to $74000 in the second before settling to a stable $49000 per quarter, which looks comfortably less than the $75000 inflows to be generated in the fourth quarter.

Table 11.2: cash flow and profit for Prosthomed.com

	1st qtr ($)	2nd qtr ($)	3rd qtr ($)	4th qtr ($)
Beginning cash balance	125000	66000	−5500	−29500
Cash inflows (income):				
Capital injected	0	0	0	0
Sales and receipts	0	2500	25000	75000
Total cash inflows	0	2500	25000	75000
Available cash balance	125000	68500	19500	45500
Cash outflows (expenses):				
Marketing and advertising	0	10000	10000	10000
Rent	4000	4000	4000	4000
Website development	25000	25000	0	0
Wages and salaries	30000	30000	30000	30000
Website support	0	5000	5000	5000
Subtotal	59000	74000	49000	49000
Ending cash balance	66000	−5500	−29500	−3500
Profit/Loss	−59000	−71500	−24000	26000

To fund the business, you injected $125000 on the first day. You expected that if you achieved your forecast sales, which rise sharply from the second quarter onwards, income would reach $102500 for the full year. Despite the expected loss in the first three quarters, the fourth quarter should post a profit that looks sustainable. From a profit and loss (P&L) point of view, the future looks promising.

Unfortunately, the firm ran out of money halfway through the year at the start of the third quarter. At that point, cash out exceeded cash available by $5500.

While this relatively modest shortfall might have been managed, the position deteriorated further in the third quarter. By then, the shortfall had increased by a further $29 500.

Suppliers were now demanding cash on delivery. This made cash flow even tighter. Other creditors were knocking on the door. The monthly rent could not be paid in full and you were issued a notice-to-quit. Staff began drifting off over non-payment of wages. Although your order book was full and growing, you didn't have the resources to fill the orders. This potentially profitable business failed by the end of the first year. What's more, the business failed before the tax office had required any payments. If things had been going better, you would have incurred a tax debt as well.

Don't forget about tax

Tax is often overlooked. It may seem odd, but the better the business is going, the bigger your goods and services tax (GST) bill is going to be. In fact, paying the government some GST every quarter is a sign of a healthy business. But it can be devastating to cash flow if you haven't budgeted for it.

It is important to understand that GST is generally calculated on accrual. That means GST is assumed to be charged when you incur the cost or send the invoice. Note that last point—when you have sent the invoice, *not* when you have received the money.

Generally, when the GST on your reported expenses is greater than the GST on your reported income, the government will refund the difference. That's good for cash flow. But the opposite occurs once you start generating net cash on an accrual basis. Then you owe the difference to the government. This can often come as a surprise. Just when you think you have moved into positive cash flow, the GST bill turns up. If a lot of your customers haven't yet paid you, then you may not have the money to pay the government.

Your primary focus

The example used in this chapter may be oversimplified, but it clearly shows how a potentially profitable business can fail due to lack of cash. This is one of the reasons—possibly the main reason—why an estimated 50 per cent of new businesses in Australia do not survive for more than five years.

Cash flow should be the primary focus of any new business and a constant theme in an existing one. While the goal is to build and maintain a profitable business, it is essential that any business plan is based on a realistic and believable cash flow budget. If you are planning a start-up, a new project or a new business plan, make this a priority. When you forecast your cash flow, stress-test your assumptions and make sure you have allowed for contingencies. Things will never go exactly as planned.

Set up a cash flow budget

If you have not set up a cash flow budget before and want to try some forecasting, download the cash flow worksheet in the reboot workshop section at <www.alanhargreaves.com> and build a budget based on your own projections. There are simple instructions for adapting the spreadsheet to your needs. Explore different scenarios. See what happens when expenses are higher, or incurred earlier. What will happen if sales fall short by 10 per cent, or if 20 per cent of your customers take 90 days instead of 30 days to pay you?

Once you are familiar with the process, you can easily begin constructing your own budget. Start stress-testing it.

Keep in mind the reasons why managing cash flow is one of your primary tasks:

▷ *You need to avoid undercapitalisation.* In the example, another $40 000 of seed capital was probably required to allow the business to survive.

▷ *You need sound forecasts to raise capital.* No potential investor, let alone a bank, will be prepared to finance your business, or its cash flow shortfall, without a believable forecast.

▷ *Cash flow analysis highlights working capital problems.* Such problems include debtor and inventory issues. When you are forecasting cash flow, the key factor is when the money is actually received, not when the invoice is issued.

▷ *Sensible forecasting avoids depending on short-term loans for long-term projects.* This has been a central problem in the recent financial crisis, when it has not been possible to roll over short-term borrowings without incurring significantly higher interest charges, or, in many cases, when it has not been possible to roll over funding at all.

▷ *You need to clearly demonstrate the ability to generate positive cash flow.* This, after all, is the fundamental hurdle you have to jump over. Examine best-case, likely and worst-case scenarios.

▷ *You must be able to meet commitments when they fall due.* The inability to fulfil payments on demand is basically the definition of insolvency. Trading while insolvent is illegal.

▷ *You need continuity of production and delivery.* Few suppliers or logistics providers will support your business if it is chronically late in paying their invoices. You cannot support your customers if your cash flow can't support your own obligations.

Check your cash flow management
Think like your accountant

Your career is going well. You've been appointed to the management committee and you are at your first meeting. The boss turns to you and says that cash is tight, then asks for any ideas you have on improving working capital management.

You answer, 'Not at the moment, but I'll look into it in my area'. You have avoided the question, but not because you don't have any ideas. Although you are great at product design and excellent at marketing, you don't have an MBA and you are not an accountant. You have avoided the question because you have no idea what your boss is talking about.

Throughout your management career you will become familiar with a range of business terms and concepts. We will cover some basic ones in this book. This is not so that you can show off at management meetings, or to keep you busy with accounting and administration. You don't have to be an expert in commercial principles, but you do need to know that they are logical and simple. Understanding them will help you make decisions.

'Working capital management' is such a term.

Understand cash flow

Open the annual report of any company and you will find a cash flow statement. It usually follows the income (or profit and loss) statement and the balance sheet. It is generally required by the accounting standards of the relevant jurisdiction and it follows a standard formula. For people not used to reading accounts, it might appear daunting, but the formula is simple.

It divides cash flows into three types, as shown in figure 12.1.

Figure 12.1: cash flow types

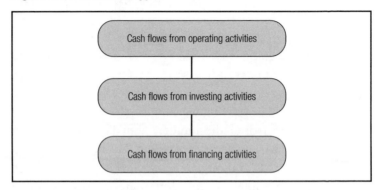

The cash flow statement simply summarises what comes in and what goes out in each activity. In short, it separates the cash that is managed around your day-to-day business from the cash that is tied up in assets and from the cash you use to fund the first two.

▷ Cash from *operating* activities is the money that comes in from sales and goes out in purchases of supplies in the course of the operations of your business. This is why it is called *working* capital. It is actually working all the time. Working capital management is the art of making sure that, at any one time, more cash is coming in than is going out — and that you use that capital as effectively as possible. Often this means not just making sure that more money is coming in, but also making sure that it is coming in sooner than it is going out.

▷ Cash from *investing* activities is cash that is spent to buy the longer term assets for the firm — the things that the firm needs to carry on its business, like land and buildings. Or, on the inflow side, it means income arising from the sale of such assets.

⇨ Cash from *financing* activities is cash received from activities such as borrowing from banks, or issuing shares, less the cash paid out in loan repayments or dividends.

These areas essentially cover all business activities related to cash. From an accounting point of view, how you collectively handle all three areas is known as cash flow management. So when you are looking for ideas on how you can manage things better, this accounting concept gives you a structure to work through.

The cash flow checklist

To carry out a quick survey of where you could improve cash flow, use the suggestions in the following paragraphs.

Operating activities

This is the core of managing working capital. To answer the question you were first asked at the hypothetical management meeting, see if you can you improve your situation in any of the following ways:

⇨ Can the rate at which money is going out be reduced? For example, can payments to suppliers be discounted, extended or exchanged for services? Can you pay less, or pay over a longer period of time?

⇨ Are inventory levels too high? Is there a case for a clearance sale? Can you schedule the delivery of and payment for supplies so that they more closely relate to the time you generate income from them?

⇨ Are receipts from customers being recovered in total and on time? Can they be recovered sooner?

⏃ Are you billing effectively? Do you issue invoices quickly and efficiently?

⏃ Can you reduce expenses by outsourcing opportunities? Can any of your products be delivered straight from supplier to customer rather than being held by you?

⏃ Can payment of incentives be scheduled differently?

⏃ Are you over-employing people? Do you need all the skills you are paying for?

⏃ Are you efficiently planning to minimise tax and manage GST payments?

Investing activities

Over time, your business can build up an asset base that doesn't necessarily match the current needs of the business. Alternatively, you may have inherited some assets that aren't required.

⏃ Do you need all your assets?

⏃ Are they all equally productive?

⏃ Should you buy or rent land and buildings?

⏃ Should you be leasing machinery rather than buying it?

Financing activities

The financing requirements of your business change over time and so does the cost of that financing.

⏃ Are you borrowing effectively and at the best rate?

⏃ Can you speed up or slow down your repayment schedule?

⏃ Is raising new equity a good avenue to explore?

⏃ If you are paying dividends, should you hold them back or reduce them?

⏃ Should you examine a dividend reinvestment plan?

Manage your cash flow

Think through your business from this accounting perspective. How can you, as a manager, adapt your operations to better fulfil the mission by optimising cash flow?

Remember that real profit can only come from operating activities. However, you can increase your available cash by using all three types of activities. We will examine some of these in more detail in the chapters ahead.

13

Manage working capital

Basic things you can do about cash flow now

Managing working capital doesn't have to be complicated. The immediate benefits come from focusing on common sense. Improving cash flow means managing the timing and the amount of inbound cash versus the timing and amount of outbound cash.

Suppliers, stock and customers

As a starting point, you should compare the terms of your credit policy with those of your suppliers. Then consider your stock (inventory) levels and possible changes to your own credit policy.

The people you pay

What exactly are the trading terms of your creditors or suppliers? Do you know them? Are they clearly specified on their invoices or in your contractual arrangement? How do their terms compare with yours?

In an ideal world, their terms would be very similar to yours. It is hard to run a business efficiently when creditors are paid on demand while your customers are free to delay payment of your receivables. However, there is usually a lag. It is largely brought about by delays in the production and delivery process. Your aim is to minimise that lag.

If this lag is causing a problem, the simplest solution is to negotiate better terms with your creditors—not just for now, but on an ongoing basis. Most suppliers will give such proposals a hearing, especially if you have developed a relationship with them. You may not get better terms, but you won't know until you ask. And you will know where you stand if you want to negotiate with alternative suppliers.

If cash is tight, can you arrange extended payment dates to get through a slow period? It is far better to approach your supplier and work through the issue rather than simply build up a reputation as a late payer.

If cash is not tight, is it worth examining a discount for early payments? Will slightly lower input costs give you a pricing edge?

The clearer you become about what these terms are, and what is possible, the easier it will be for you to balance incomings and outgoings.

Your stock levels

Inventory costs money. Managing it can save money. Do that by asking three basic questions:

1 How much do I have?
2 How much do I need?
3 When do I need it?

One of the most famous examples of effective inventory management is the system used by Toyota. Currently, they are the best and most profitable vehicle manufacturer in the world. Yes, even now. Most would agree that the core of their success is the manufacture of cars that deliver genuinely high quality at a competitive price. A key factor behind their competitive pricing is the *kanban* system. *Kanban* is Japanese for the original card system Toyota used to keep track of the answers to those three questions. It is generally now known as just-in-time (JIT) inventory management. Essentially, Toyota carefully planned and monitored the input requirements of their production schedules using the card system. They shared this information with their suppliers to ensure that parts were delivered just before they were needed and therefore the amount of capital tied up in inventories was managed to the absolute minimum. They have continued to follow the principles of this system.

Any business can do the same. JIT inventory management reduces the cost of capital by cutting the amount of cash needed to maintain the business. In Toyota's case, it has increased their cost advantage. Their suppliers are happy because they too can manage their own businesses more efficiently. This collaboration builds loyalty into supplier relationships—something that can be quite helpful in difficult times.

The people who pay you

When you compared your credit policy with those of your suppliers, you may have noticed a number of differences. When people do this exercise, they often find that those with the most sensibly specified policies are those that you regard as some of the better run businesses.

This is not surprising. You may produce and market an excellent product or service, but your business will only be successful if you promptly collect the money you are owed. We will talk more about credit policy in chapter 14. For now, look at a few simple things:

⚏ Can you bring your own terms more into line with the requirements of your creditors?

⚏ Are there areas where you can legitimately ask for cash on delivery (COD)?

⚏ Is there room for requiring a deposit on acceptance of an order?

⚏ Can you trade off earlier and definite delivery for prompter payment?

Take some action

Examine the trading terms for your debtors and creditors in tandem to help you identify where your own process can be streamlined. Assess your inventory. You may not require the sophisticated JIT practices of Toyota, but the principle is the same and so is the outcome: you tie up less capital for a shorter period of time.

Lastly, ensure the basic things are done properly. Bill on time. Present invoices very clearly and as soon as they are due. Offer every convenient means of payment that does not increase your cost of collection. Make the due date very clear. Make it clear what is due and what is overdue. Be equally clear about what you will charge on overdue amounts and when you will charge it. Then do so.

Review your business practices on this comparative basis and make the overall equation clear in your mind. Efficient capital management is key to ensuring a business survives the hard times. Equally, it is this sort of fine-tuning that places the firm in the strongest position to take advantage of buoyant conditions.

14

Develop a clear credit policy

It's more than just collecting money

So far in part II, you have looked at simple things you can do to improve working capital management. In chapter 13, you compared your own credit policy with those of your creditors. Do you know the most common outcome of that exercise? It reveals that many businesses don't really have a credit policy at all, or if they do, they don't have the right one, or if they have the right one, they don't really follow it.

However, managing receivables—that is, money owed to you—is fundamental to success. You might be great at managing the expense side, but what about the income? Remember that a credit policy is not just about collecting money. Having a clearly defined and maintained credit policy will:

⮒ send a signal to your customers that you are a professionally run enterprise
⮒ enable you to more accurately forecast your cash flow
⮒ allow you to manage your finances more efficiently
⮒ help you to handle issues with problem payers.

Simple steps for building a workable policy

Consider the following steps when building your credit policy. Remember to set realistic goals and to compare your terms with industry standards.

Step1: Develop your terms

Develop what you think are fair and reasonable payment terms for your clients and products. Then assess these terms in light of what you found when examining your capital management and how your business is best funded. What will work for you?

Step 2: Compare your terms

Compare these terms with industry practices in your sector and review them if necessary. Start with baseline, or standard, conditions. These could be that all customers are invoiced within 7 days of delivery or purchase order, and invoices are payable within 7 days of receipt. In an ideal (but unrealistic) world, this means you will be paid no later than 14 days after sale or delivery.

Step 3: Rank your customers

Next, examine your customer base and rank them all by their size, their importance to you, their payment history and any other factors you consider relevant to your business. Grade them into A, B and C, where A are preferred customers, B are standard customers and C are customers whom you would rather avoid (or from whom you would demand payment prior to delivery).

Step 4: Check credit

If queries arise in developing the ranking in step 3, undertake a credit check for relevant customers. If it makes commercial sense, make such a check a requirement for opening an account with any customer. Ask for references and follow them up. This process alone will gradually improve the quality of your customer base.

If you find you have particularly difficult debtors, find out more about who you are dealing with. Check the credit histories of their directors and owners. Whatever you decide when you are setting things up, make sure that it is stated as policy and that the relevant box can be ticked before they open an account with you.

Step 5: Rank your products

Rank your range of products and services. Do some need such specialist handling that a deposit is required prior to accepting the order? Does it make sense to provide others only on a COD basis? Can some services be moved onto a predictable payment plan, such as retainers or maintenance charges? Are they the core drivers of your business? Should they be treated differently?

In ranking your products, stay as close as possible to your standard terms. Moving away from this would only be for special items where, say, a high ranking would mean payment as early as possible, and a low one would be supported by normal or extended terms.

Step 6: Adjust your terms

Examine how you might adjust your baseline terms in line with your products and customers' needs. Don't overcomplicate this. Try to keep it simply to normal terms and preferred terms, plus a special category where COD, deposits or problem customers are handled.

Step 7: Adjust your penalties

Do the same with charging penalties on overdue payments. Make the rate fair and reasonable and make it apply after a sensible period of time. Call it an administration charge because, partly, that's what it is. Also, make it reflect your own cost of money. Legally, you probably can't charge interest, but customers will relate more clearly to an administration fee if it reflects what the bank is charging you for your overdraft. This, after all, is what you are paying to support a customer's late payment.

Step 8: Write your terms

Write down your standard terms and conditions. Include them in your invoice or contractual arrangements with clients. Do not include preferred terms. Leave these for negotiation with clients who demand them or deserve them. When offering them, make it clear to them that they are receiving preferential treatment, even if they are in the majority.

Step 9: Monitor your debtors

Monitor your debtor performance. Put someone in charge of this. This is essential, even if it is you. You must have a system whereby overdue accounts are flagged on a regular basis. You need a weekly report from the credit manager showing who is late, who is on time and who is early. Patterns will become clear over time and problem debtors will become apparent.

Step 10: Follow up payments

Have definite rules in relation to late payers that follow a definite sequence and that call for a particular action at each stage. For example, decide at what point you or your credit manager will call the customer requesting payment. On that call, you might offer to waive additional charges if the account is cleared within the next period. Only do this once. Set a date after which the account will not be supplied and after which an administration fee will be charged.

Step 11: Be reasonable

Some customers may be going through temporary difficulties and you may be able to assist them with a payment plan. Many will be grateful if you help them through a seasonal fluctuation or an unforeseen development. This will pay off in future loyalty. Don't let it become a habit, but accommodate those cases that you feel are legitimate.

Step 12: Stay firm

By all means have discussions with problem payers, but once you decide on the next action, do not backtrack. Make each step very clear. If you say you are going to take further action to recover the debt, do what you say.

The results

Most customers will appreciate a clearly defined credit policy. They too need to know what their obligations are. It may mean that some customers will leave. Be aware that you cannot afford some of them. Your customer base will become more reliable if ongoing problem payers become other companies' problems. Remember the saying, 'If you lend someone $50 and never see that person again, the money may have been well spent'.

Develop a range of financing options
Review the cost of your asset base

So far, you have focused on working capital. That's the cheapest and fastest form of funding. If you can optimise your operating cash flow, you will reduce the amount of capital you need to employ in the business. That means you will have either a lower overdraft or more money in the bank.

Either way, it's a good result. Money always has a cost or a return, be it the interest you pay to borrow it or the interest you earn from a deposit. Every dollar you add to cash flow through prudent management will either save you interest payments or bring you interest income. That will translate straight to the bottom line.

For the active manager, adjustment of working capital is also the quickest option of funding. When they put their minds to it, most managers can shave inventory, extend payment terms with suppliers or press for earlier completion of outstanding receivables. But there is an additional perspective on finance that comes from an accountant's view of cash flow. It leads us to compare the cost of different sources of capital.

Funding from investing and financing activities

Cash from operations is the least expensive funding option. You don't pay anything for it. However, as we move into the other two categories of cash flow—cash from investing activities and cash from financing activities—we need to consider the cost of funding.

Businesses have garage sales too

A review of your investing activities can reveal some low-cost options of sourcing funds. Many businesses have so-called legacy assets—plant, machinery, land or other resources that no longer contribute greatly to core operations. There is a lot to be said for the business equivalent of a garage sale. It is often surprising how much money can be saved or raised, or how much space can be made available for other activities, through a determined attempt to remove asset clutter. Just as earlier processes looked at clearing away counterproductive management styles, a thorough review of your asset base can lead to a physically cleaner, leaner and more efficient business.

In this chapter, there are two tasks. The first is to examine your asset base and look for items that are available for disposal, trade-in, upgrade or sale. In this process, don't ignore the option of discontinuing unproductive or unprofitable operations. Disposing of such low-hanging fruit might yield a good result in the short term.

Asset management plans

The second task in your asset review is to look at how your assets are financed and what alternatives are available. Investigate the range of options for all aspects of your business. Management needs to know what is available to support existing or new initiatives. Each option has advantages and disadvantages and each has a different cost.

You don't need to decide which option to choose now, but you need to familiarise yourself with what is available. You are probably already aware of and understand some options. To find out about others, you might need to do some internet surfing. In many cases, one telephone call will lead you to an eager financial broker who is more than willing to walk you through a particular product and how it can be arranged.

Look at some options

Consider these possibilities:

▷ Organise well-planned asset disposals (rather than fire/garage sales) based on your long-term business plans.

▷ Sell non-core parts of your business and replace them with outsourced services.

▷ Offer some of your own processes as an outsourced service and put them in a separately financed—and saleable—subsidiary.

▷ Seek vendor financing from suppliers.

▷ Negotiate discounted payment terms for inputs.

▷ Examine leasing options for existing or new plant.

▷ Look for contra opportunities with suppliers or customers.

▷ Investigate peer-to-peer funding.

▷ Factor your receivables to raise cash. Factoring is a system of selling your receivables to a third party. It usually involves a discount, but it can be a quick way of raising funds if required.

▷ Examine debtors who are seriously delinquent. You may be able to sell some of these aged receivables for a certain amount of cents in the dollar.

▷ Use a debt collection agency to try to recover aged receivables on your behalf. Allow them a commission on the amount that is recovered only.

▷ Renegotiate existing credit lines or explore new ones. Let your bank know that you are always open to alternatives, including changing banks.

▷ Examine equity funding alternatives. Initial public offerings or convertible bonds may not be on your current radar, but examining the options available will broaden your perspective on the best means of funding your business expansion.

The price of each of these strategies is different, and they are often difficult to compare. Outsourcing releases cash but can sometimes raise costs. Leasing incurs interest, but tax savings may offset the expense. Discount arrangements for input purchases lowers costs but may limit your flexibility in choice of supplier. Banks may provide loans, but the covenants they require may restrict your activities.

Nonetheless, set yourself the task of reviewing your options. Examine each of these alternatives and become familiar with them. In the next few chapters, you will look at assessing these and other options in financial terms.

16

Work with banks

Be clear about your bank's agenda

Banks get a lot of bad press. They are accused of profiteering, of insensitivity to the needs of borrowers, of not providing cheap and reasonable credit to the business sector, plus a whole range of other questionable practices.

These views are largely fuelled by poor service experiences and by some banks charging irritating fees. The truth is, the banking system is fundamental to the successful functioning of the economy; conservative management of this system is better for the economy.

The sub-prime crisis made this clear. Banks lent money to borrowers who could not afford to repay them. They weren't prime borrowers; they were sub-prime. Australia had its own equivalent, 'low-doc loans', for which borrowers did not have to rigorously prove their ability to service a mortgage. What's more, they could borrow more than a property was worth. None of these practices could be called conservative.

What happens when it goes wrong

When the global financial crisis hit, the sub-prime default rate skyrocketed. It did this particularly aggressively in the US, because under US law, you can default on your mortgage and just walk away. It is up to the bank to recover what it can by selling the property. That leads to a huge amount of property for sale, which only depresses prices further and starts to put pressure on prime borrowers as well. When banks aren't conservative, everybody suffers.

So it is actually a positive move if banks are no longer making mortgages easy to procure. That's certainly more in line with the bank's mission (to optimise returns to shareholders over time). And virtually all of us are shareholders. Remember what happened to Citibank shareholders. Prior to the crisis, they were holding shares valued at US$55 and were receiving dividends. Two years later the shares traded under US$1 and paid no dividend.

If you can't see why that should be important to you, imagine having a large number of Citibank shares in your superannuation scheme. What would have happened to your balance? Luckily, you are probably holding Commonwealth Bank shares (like just about everyone else in Australia who is in a superannuation scheme). These shares were trading around A$55 prior to the crisis, and quickly recovered to a price about that level—and these shares never stopped paying dividends.

Australia escaped the GFC relatively unscathed because the sub-prime or low-doc practices didn't get quite so out of hand. Also, borrowers have to take responsibility for their mortgages—they can't just walk away. The conservatism of the Australian banks, and the regulatory environment in which they operate, meant they remained some of the few AAA-rated banks in the world. Even if you don't like your bank, that's a good result, not a bad one.

Banks are commercial animals

The only way to view a bank is to see it as a commercial entity, not as a social service. That does not mean banks shouldn't be socially responsible; however, they are a business just like any other. They have to buy inputs and sell outputs.

Banks don't have a free rein with the prices of those inputs and outputs. People forget that banks are borrowers too. They have their own suppliers in the form of depositors, capital markets and inter-bank lenders. For a price, those entities supply the raw material from which the banks fashion their own products, which are known as loans. In turn, for a price, the banks sell those products to you, the customers. When money is tight, the banks have to pay a higher price for it, and so do you.

The price in this case is the interest rate. And the general level of interest rates is rarely determined by the banks either. It is determined by the business cycle and the market price for money.

Factors that affect interest rates

There are various components that influence a bank's interest rates:

➪ *Official rates.* Your bank doesn't decide these — that's the job of central banks. Central banks are not commercial banks. They are more like referees. They are not meant to take sides with either lenders or borrowers, although they are often accused of both. Their main objectives are things like controlling inflation or maintaining economic stability. Like referees, they can get it wrong. But also like referees, they have the last say on official rates.

➪ *Risk-free rates.* These are usually the rates on government bonds (on the odd assumption that governments don't fail). And governments don't set these rates either. When they sell bonds, they have to pay whatever interest rate the market decides. When money is tight, governments have to pay up too.

➪ *Rates in capital markets.* When banks need more capital, they have to buy it in those markets. If money is tight, they too have to pay up. They usually pay more than the risk-free rate because banks can, and do, fail.

So the cost of money is affected by lots of elements that the banks have little or no power over.

What the banks do decide

What *is* determined by commercial banks is the interest rate differential (or the risk component) of the rate you are charged. This is the margin you will have to pay over and above official or market rates to borrow the money. That margin reflects various risks: the risk of you failing; the risk of the bank failing; and the risk of the economy failing.

Imagine risk-free rates are around 5 per cent. Your bank and the economy are in reasonable shape. In that case, suppliers might lend your bank money at 5 per cent plus a margin of, say, 1.5 per cent. Now we have 6.5 per cent. Let's also say you are a reasonable credit risk and that when lending to you, the bank will add 1.5 per cent to their cost of funds, and therefore you will borrow money at 8 per cent.

The agenda is never stable

If conditions remained stable, you could plan accordingly and continue your business. The problem arises when the bank's agenda changes for reasons beyond your and their control. A classic example of this was the withdrawal of car dealer financing in the wake of the sub-prime crisis.

Car dealers hold a range of stock in their showrooms in order to market their vehicles. They do not purchase this inventory outright. Rather than tie up funds, they finance it externally. A dominant player in this sector was GE Capital, a well-regarded global financial institution.

During the crisis, dealer financing became too risky for GE. It wasn't really GE who brought this about. It didn't matter how reliable or profitable the dealers were; GE found it increasingly difficult to raise funds at a reasonable price from its own suppliers because they saw it as risky business, especially in the middle of a global crisis. Suppliers raised the margins on lending to GE, who in turn found the cost of capital rising sharply. GE could only address this by reducing its exposure to car dealers.

GE's response was in fact to eliminate this exposure entirely. Suddenly, previously solvent car dealers were subject to acute financial distress. Alternatives had to be found. Makeshift programs were put in place. Their cost of funds skyrocketed. Some managed. Some didn't.

In short, the financial rug was pulled from under them at exactly the time when they most needed funding to weather one of the toughest recessions in the post-war period.

This can happen to you

So the situation is always going to be fluid. What can you do about it? The only management options you have are to take steps to improve your relationship with your bank or to find alternative funding. Think about the following options.

Develop alternative funding strategies

Consider the strategies outlined in chapter 15. Work through these plans now, not when you are forced to. What would you do if your bank pulled your credit line? How exposed are you?

Examine your relationship with your shareholders

You do not have to be a publicly listed company to have a rights issue or to sell equity in your business. In some cases, the latter can form part of a strong relationship with other key stakeholders in your business.

Shareholders are also a source of loan funds, and they often make better lending partners than banks. Investigate shareholder loans.

Choose a bank, service it and stick with it

While there is an argument for shopping around for credit lines, if you are going to require bank facilities over a long term, you are better off developing a strong relationship with a preferred partner. You need one that you are comfortable with and one where you can develop a working relationship with your account manager. He or she must be senior enough to argue your case and able to become familiar with you and your business.

Go out of your way to support that manager. Remember that this person has a job to hold down too. Supply information about your business and how it is going. Discuss potential problems, share your ideas and ask for solutions. Get the bank's perspective on your business. What areas do they find less risky? Does that suggest products and services you could build on that have a stronger credit rating and therefore have greater value in the long term?

Having said all that, keep an open communication with some of your bank's direct competitors—and let your bank know that you do.

Use debt scientifically

A problem that often creeps up on firms is the use of credit lines for non-specified purposes. The overdraft that was put in place to carry the firm through seasonal fluctuations or unforeseen events starts to be drawn down for everyday operating expenses. Rather than remaining focused on costs and staying financially lean, the business creeps towards dependence on a certain level of borrowings. But as the business cycle moves, the cost of servicing the debt shifts. Suddenly it becomes a serious burden at a time when spare cash is being squeezed. Or worse still, the credit line is called in and the firm simply doesn't have the resources to cover it. Invariably, it happens all at once.

If you borrow money, borrow it for a specific purpose, match it against a specific plan, implement the plan and pay back the money.

This does not mean there is never a case for gearing up. High leverage is not always unintentional and, fully stress-tested, a geared strategy can underwrite very strong returns. However, the negative aspects generally develop from actions taken during good times, when the boundaries of the stress-test were drawn too optimistically.

Keep yourself afloat

During the GFC, excessive gearing was the undoing of many great ideas. The crisis was a 'perfect storm'. It proved that everything could go wrong at once. You need to consider alternative funding strategies and relationships with shareholders not just as a means of coping with difficult times. They are best applied ahead of those times to manage debt rather than grow it.

The central equation behind many private equity failures was to aggressively manage working capital—by squeezing the receivables/payables equation, running down inventories and selling off 'non-core' balance sheet assets. There is nothing inherently wrong with such initiatives. The problem was that the goal was not the efficient management of the business but the generation of more cash in order to borrow more money. It was the consequent indebtedness that killed them. Don't let it happen to you.

17
Understand the cost of capital

Can I make money from this?

My father was a retailer and a trader. He had strong merchandising skills and an eye for goods he could move quickly. If a trade made sense to him, he would do it on borrowed funds.

These were handy skills amid the shortages of post-war Australia in the 1950s. If he spotted a scarce roll of carpet in a warehouse, he would calculate his markup, compare it with his overdraft rate, buy the carpet and then sell it on as quickly as he could. The principle was simple: 'If you can't do it with someone else's money, it's probably not worth doing.'

The cost and value of money

Today, people use more complicated words to explain this. Most MBA programs will have units on calculating 'return on investment' (ROI), 'net present value' (NPV), 'internal rate of return' (IRR) and 'weighted average cost of capital' (WACC).

Don't be deterred by the terminology. The principles are no different from my father's 1950s arithmetic. For him, it was common sense: he had to get a return that was better than his overdraft rate, and the quicker he turned over his inventory, the sooner he would achieve that return and the sooner he could do it again.

Those two principles—the cost of money and its value over time—are central to modern corporate finance theory.

The cost of your own money

There is no point in undertaking an enterprise if you would be better off doing something else. Your view of 'better off' may vary, depending on your personal preferences for a certain lifestyle or your goal of reaching a financial target over time. However, you will still need to look at the most efficient way of achieving your aim, and you will want to be confident that the result will be worth the trouble.

Start with the basic investment decision of choosing your 'risk appetite'. This is to do with how much stress you want. You have $100 000 to invest. You don't want to lose it and you'd like to make some return on it. If you can put it in the bank and earn 5 per cent over 12 months, that is your most hassle-free and best sleep-at-night option. For you, that is the nearest thing to the 'risk-free rate' referred to in chapter 16. It is also effectively the cost of that capital. If you invest it in something else, you are giving up that 5 per cent. There is no point in doing something else unless it can jump over that hurdle. So even if you are cashed up, there is a cost to using the cash you have.

The cost of someone else's money

If you don't have the cash and you have to borrow it, the cost of your capital will rise because there is now a risk that you won't pay it back. Whoever is lending you the money knows they can always get the risk-free rate. So if they are going to lend it to you, they will have to add a margin to cover the additional risk they are taking on you. That's called the 'risk component'. Suppose your risk component is 3.75 per cent and the risk-free rate is 5 per cent. The cost of this form of debt can be calculated using this simple formula:

$$\text{Cost of debt} = \text{risk-free rate} + \text{risk component}$$
$$= 5 \text{ per cent} + 3.75 \text{ per cent}$$
$$= 8.75 \text{ per cent}$$

Clearly, whatever you are planning to invest in, whether with your own money or someone else's, you will need to generate a return that is higher than the relevant rate.

The cost of equity

The most expensive source of capital is equity. That is because it is the most risky. It is also the most difficult to calculate because, unlike interest rates, the rate of return on equity is largely unknown until it is achieved.

Equity costs at least the risk-free rate (because the money can always be put in a risk-free deposit) plus the 'risk premium'. This premium relates to the risk involved in the project or business it is invested in. This is usually higher than the risk component in the cost of debt because, basically, with equity you have the opportunity to lose everything. With start-ups, people often do.

Think of this as being like buying shares on margin (a practice in which it is also quite easy to lose everything). You will pay interest on what you borrow to buy the shares and you will want a return on the shares that covers not only the lending rate but also the risk you are taking. The equation for the cost of equity is:

Cost of equity = risk-free rate + equity risk premium

For example, if you borrowed $100 000 for 12 months and over that period the shares you bought increased by 16.25 per cent, the implied equity risk premium (using our examples so far) would be 11.25 per cent, as shown in this equation:

Cost of equity = risk-free rate + equity risk premium
16.25 per cent = 5 per cent + equity risk premium
Equity risk premium = 11.25 per cent

Because the cost of equity is forecast, it is invariably rubbery. Still, it must be considered a cost of capital because if that capital was earning 16.25 per cent, it wouldn't make sense to invest it in something else unless that investment would earn more than 16.25 per cent.

There are many indicators you can draw on when working out equity risk premiums in your sector. We will touch on these in later chapters. The point is that you need to have a view on what your hurdle rate is when assessing your own business success, or when assessing any new initiatives, be they organic growth projects, taking over a competitor, launching an entirely new business or selling your own.

On average, what is money costing you?

To evaluate how much money is costing, the most logical measure to use is the weighted average cost of capital (WACC). It essentially means what it says: if you take the capital (both debt and equity) that you have invested in your business, then, on average, what does it cost?

Using the above example, ignore tax and imagine a simplified business with $100000 of equity and a $100000 overdraft, fully drawn. The equity has a cost of 16.25 per cent; assume the overdraft costs 8.75 per cent. The WACC is therefore the average of 16.25 per cent and 8.75 per cent, which is 12.5 per cent. For the business to make any sense at all, it should be earning at least 12.5 per cent on its capital. Any new investment in the business needs to at least meet that hurdle rate.

On average, are you creating value?

This brings us to the last rate we want to consider— the actual return on invested capital. In other words, regardless of your WACC, what are you actually making out of what you have invested?

A principle of corporate finance theory is that the greater the spread between your WACC and your actual return on invested capital, the greater is the value of your business. There is nothing special about this. It simply brings us back to where we started: if you can make more money using someone else's money, you are creating value. The more you can do that, the higher is the value of what you have created.

A simple way of looking at this is to work out what you think you could sell your business for and divide your net profit by that number. That's your actual return.

For example, if you think your business is worth $1 million and your net profit is $100 000, your actual return is 10 per cent. If you undertake a new project that will return less than that, you will destroy value. Your overall rate of return will be reduced. If you can develop a project that will return more, you will create value.

Understand your decisions

The purpose of this chapter is not to investigate financial theory, but to explain the arithmetic principles behind business decisions, many of which you probably already make intuitively, just as my father did. However, remember to put some science into your thinking, and work out the hurdle rate for your business. What return is required to make commercial sense out of what you are doing?

Understand the time value of money

What is the future result worth today?

I often come across small businesses, especially franchises, where the proprietors would be better off if they just put their money in the bank. Too often, people value their businesses on the basis of the salaries the businesses can afford to pay them. If you buy a franchise for, say, $300 000 and all you are focused on is taking home a salary of $50 000, you are probably in that category. You need to be making a risk-adjusted return on your $300 000 *and* taking home $50 000.

This is the case with a lot of small businesses. Given the incredibly long hours and the high level of stress involved in managing them, you should consider investing your capital elsewhere, getting a job and avoiding an early grave.

As we said in chapter 17, the value of your money is not just the *amount* you have tied up in the business — it depends on how much that money has cost you and on how long you have it tied up. The time value of money is often ignored by businesspeople and investors, yet it has a huge impact on the value you create.

People often fall in love with their assets or base their decisions on fantasy. You see it often in the property market. Owners can hold off selling a property for years, waiting for a price they have an emotional attachment to. But money in the hand has value. Every time they reject lower offers, they need to acknowledge what return they could have received on that money, even if that return is relatively low.

I have a friend who wanted to sell his investment unit for $500 000. It was an unrealistic price at the time. He rejected several offers over three years. The first offer was $450 000. He eventually got his price, but if he had invested the $450 000 in a term deposit at 6.85 per cent (the going rate over that period), it would have compounded into approximately $550 000 by the time of the sale. Even taking the most conservative view of his tax planning, he would have been ahead had he made the early sale.

This leads us to the concept of 'present value' (PV). It is simply the reverse of the example just given. To achieve $550 000 in three years' time at an interest rate of 6.85 per cent per annum, you need to invest $450 000 now.

Take account of time

In business, you can take the notion of PV further by calculating 'net present value' (NPV). This is a useful way of working out the value of a project or a new product or service. Basically, it tells you whether it is worth the trouble.

Assume you intend to offer a new service. It will take an investment of $50 000 to set up the necessary infrastructure. Each year it will generate $20 000 and will cost $5000 to run. In other words, it will net $15 000 each year, or a 30 per cent return on your $50 000 investment. Not too bad, you might say.

However, that capital you are tying up *should* earn a return, and because of the time value of money, that $15 000 will be worth less each year. Exactly how much less is a function of your financial hurdle rate—like the cost of capital, or your WACC, as described in chapter 17.

Walk through the very simple mathematics. The rate used in calculating NPV is known as the discount rate—that is, it is the rate at which you should discount your money over time, because that's what it costs.

Let's say the discount rate is 10 per cent. On the first day of business, you will have negative cash flow of $50 000, because you have invested that in the project. It's gone.

At the end of the first year, you will have generated cash flow of $15 000. But it is not really worth that by then, because it could have been earning 10 per cent. Its PV will be $13 636.

Think of this as being similar to the real estate example. If interest rates are 10 per cent and you want $15 000 in one year's time, you need to invest $13 636, because 10 per cent interest on $13 636 over 12 months is $1364. Adding these amounts gives $15 000. You can work this out on your calculator, but if you want to take a short cut, search for present value tables on the internet and apply them, or quicker still, use the NPV function on your spreadsheet software.

In the second year, you will earn another $15 000, but that is two years away at 10 per cent per year. So its value to you now, its PV, is only $12 396. This process will continue for the following years.

To calculate the NPV of the project, add up all the PVs and subtract them from your initial investment to see if it is positive. As shown in table 18.1, this project starts to have positive NPV at the end of year 5. (Note that the PVs in table 18.1 are given to the nearest dollar, and because of this rounding their sum is not exactly the same as the NPV shown.)

Table 18.1: calculation of NPV

End of year	Cash flow	Compound discount rate	PV (to the nearest dollar)
0	−$50 000	0%	−$50 000
1	$15 000	10%	$13 636
2	$15 000	21%	$12 396
3	$15 000	33%	$11 269
4	$15 000	46%	$10 245
5	$15 000	61%	$9313
			NPV = $6861

If you think this project has a five-year life and you take into account the time value of money, your investment seems to be worth it. However, when the NPV is less than zero, it is not. If the NPV is zero, the project is basically a break-even endeavour. If your WACC is 10 per cent (that is, the same as in the example), the positive result means you have created value for your business — you have generated a positive spread between your cost of capital and your return on invested capital.

Compare your potential returns

Be aware that a positive NPV does not necessarily mean you should go ahead with your venture. If you have alternative projects you could invest the $50 000 in, run NPV calculations on them and see if the results are better. Test whether investing more in your existing operations rather than starting new ones is a better use of your capital. Also remember that your investment does not need to be in your own business. For a reality check, compare your NPV returns with those achievable in other businesses or investments completely unrelated to yours.

Decide on the discount rate

By now you are probably asking whether all this depends on the so-called discount rate. It does. That is why you need to develop your own sense for what is a reasonable rate for your business and your expectations.

You might decide to undertake a diligent analysis of your WACC and use that as your benchmark. It may be simply the rate you get on stress-free, relatively risk-free term deposits. It may be the government bond rate. It may be your overdraft rate. You might want to build in a premium to cover changes in interest rates over time. If the project is risky, the discount rate needs to increase to accommodate the risk.

Know your return

It may be that you simply love your business. You don't, won't or can't do anything else, and you are happy with a moderate return if it means you can keep on doing what you like doing. Nonetheless, you still need to be aware of what that moderate return is.

This re-emphasises the point made in chapter 17: you need to have some measure of your business performance. You will make far sounder business decisions if you know exactly what hurdle you have to get over to make it worth your while being in business in the first place. It will help you scientifically assess new ideas, make ongoing decisions (such as whether to rent or buy, own or lease) and evaluate major options (such as whether to hold or to sell your business).

Know what your business is worth

Whaf's your selling price?

Imagine someone walks into your office tomorrow and wants to buy your business. This person has the cash and is ready to deal. You receive an offer. The price is several times what you make from the business each year. It is certainly more than the capital you have put into it. The person would like a response today. What will you say?

Most likely nothing. You will have to think about it. Most people do, because they often haven't thought about it at all. A hardworking entrepreneur gets on with the business. The focus is on the P&L, the cash flow and maybe the balance sheet. The value of what you have created is always out in the future: won't it be great when ...

There is nothing wrong with that, but if the focus is only on the bottom line, you are missing out on the advantages of taking a bigger view of your business. Businesses build worth. They create assets, grow brands, establish income streams and generate market share. All these things can be valued. How much value do you want to create? How will you get there?

You can set a target for the value of your business and plan for it. Don't wait for someone to walk into your office and make an offer.

Valuation and growth

Valuation can be a great tool. It can assist your investment decisions. It can clarify your prospects. It can tell you when to get in deeper, or when to get out, which product lines to grow, or which ones to exit. It's essential if your want to raise money, and even more so if you want to sell.

Let's look first at the big reasons why valuation matters. Ownership of a business rarely stands still. Even dedicated founders who nurtured their businesses from scratch eventually retire. The business might then be sold, bequeathed or passed on to family. Whatever the case, ownership will change.

Even before then, the business may go through different structures to achieve success. Equity partners might be introduced to pay for expansion. If the enterprise was funded by other shareholders from the start, they might be bought out. The firm could go public, take over a competitor, merge with another business or be taken over itself. Ownership is dynamic and it is part of the process of wealth creation.

At any one of these points in the life cycle of your business, you will face the crucial question: what is it worth? You cannot set a price for issuing new shares, merging with another business or selling to an acquirer without knowing your value.

Valuation as a planning tool

Valuation is more than just a sales price. It provides an alternative approach to making strategic decisions. Once you understand the value of your whole firm, you can break it down into its constituent parts. Are there independent business units that can stand alone? What are their individual values? Do you see their worth rising or falling? Which candidate deserves more resources? It will not be the one that is facing a flat or falling value. That is a candidate for disposal. Its sale can raise funds to channel into areas with a more positive outlook.

Regular monitoring of brands, products or income streams will keep you aware of the price the business environment is putting on your efforts. It will help you to decide what areas of business you should pursue more aggressively. They will change over time, just as, say, fixed line networks of major telcos now command a lower value than mobile telephony, or where higher margin focaccias provide income streams that are valued more highly than those of ham sandwiches.

Use valuation to check on depreciating assets. Will they shortly be worthless, or can they be enhanced? Should they be sold now? Would leasing them make better sense?

What's the easiest way to do this?

A simple approach to valuation

The quickest reference point is a so-called multiple. There are plenty of others, but this is the simplest. Stock market prices provide multiples. If shares are trading at $7 and each share earns $1, the multiple is 7. Check the market multiple for the industry you are in. Alternatively, call a business broker and ask what multiples businesses are selling for in your sector. There is no single number, but a few research calls will give you a reasonable range of where the market is. They can go from zero to 20, but most are in the middle.

Once you have that range, look at your own business. Where does your multiple sit in the range? Are you a premium firm that will command the top of the range, or are you much like the others?

Next, examine the components of your business. Not all earnings are valued at the same level. Different income streams have different characteristics. Some will be very recurrent in nature. These will command a higher multiple because of their dependability. Others will be more volatile and will be valued lower.

The market will often put a high price on areas with strong growth possibilities, or on firms that have a strong competitive advantage over the opposition and are in areas with high barriers to entry. Identifiable growth prospects or entrenched market positions can often command premium multiples. It is simply easier for someone to buy your business than reinvent it. This is the logic behind many takeovers and it pushes multiples higher.

What can you do?

What income streams—existing and potential—are you able to develop to command the highest multiples? Consider targeted leverage, greater focus, new marketing initiatives, product improvements or new products altogether. What, really, is the full potential of your business?

There are some dangers here. Anyone can tell you of good businesses being driven into the ground with excessive leverage and expansion strategies aimed at quickly producing high valuations. Equally, there are many cases where the application of valuation thinking has transformed struggling firms into vibrant and highly valued businesses. The latter is what you want to be.

Look at what your company is worth now and what you want it to be worth in the future. Let's stay with our simple example. Assume that the price investors are prepared to pay is around seven times the net earnings of the firm. In other words, if the company's net profit after tax is $500 000, the value of the company would be $3 500 000.

What do you want it to be? What can it be?

Say you want to retire with $7 million. In that case, you have two options. You need to double your earnings, or shift the firm towards activities that would encourage the market to value it at a higher multiple. By looking at the values of individual components, you can identify where your effort should be focused.

Valuation focus: a short exercise

Spend an hour researching and writing your answers to the following questions. Make your responses the agenda for your next think tank meeting.

1   What is the range of multiples for your business?
2   Who are your best people? If you really gave them a chance, what could they create? What could you create?
3   What are your best products or services? What could you do to make them the standouts in their sectors?
4   What is your firm's strongest skill? What resources could you use or enhance to take your firm to its absolute potential?
5   What is your strongest market opportunity? What could you do to really take advantage of it?
6   What is the strongest scenario for your business? Forecast each of the following areas and outline the really bold action you could take to dramatically lift the value of your company in each area:

   - the trends in your customers' demand
   - the likely direction of your competitors
   - the impact of new technology
   - the outlook for each of your products and services.

When you have completed these questions, estimate what you think your business is worth now, and what it could be worth in the future. Then, if someone walks into your office and makes an offer, you'll know what to say: 'I'm not interested' or 'Let's talk'.

Know how to work with multiples

What numbers should you use?

In chapter 19, we looked at why you should understand the value of your business. But not everyone will come up with the same amount.

Valuation is a rubbery concept. The figures can differ markedly depending on the method you use. Some valuations are useful in certain negotiations; others are widely accepted in your industry or in the marketplace generally. You need to be familiar with the basic ones.

The price/earnings ratio

Begin with the simple multiple we used in chapter 19. Its formal name is the 'price/earnings ratio' (P/E ratio). It's a simple notion. Its popularity reflects its easy use in monitoring shares on the stock market. To revise this concept, consider the following example.

Say there are 1 million shares in a company and that company posts a profit after tax of $1 million. The earnings per share (EPS) is the net profit divided by the number of shares; in this case, the EPS is $1.

The P/E ratio is the price divided by the earnings. If the shares are trading for $7 each, the P/E ratio is 7 ($7 divided by $1). In other words, the stock market is valuing the firm at 7 times its net profit or, in total, $7 million (that is, the total number of shares on issue multiplied by the share price).

If you are aiming to list your firm publicly, you should monitor its P/E ratio. For example, if your goal is to have a certain valuation at the end of five years, many of your business decisions would take into account the impact on your EPS. These decisions would include your policies on depreciation, tax planning, leasing, renting, asset disposal, outsourcing and so on.

These are important decisions in the efficient running of a business. They also impact heavily on the presentation of your financials and reflect your capital structure (in this case, one made up of issued shares). This is one reason why the P/E ratio is important to stock market investors. They are not in control of these decisions. They simply have to assess the information available to ordinary shareholders, such as the EPS.

Other measures

For management, the entrepreneur or the controlling share-holder, it can be more important to build the value of the firm through growth of operations and the cash they produce. In this case, you need to look at different multiples.

Common measures include an array of acronyms such as EBT (earnings before taxes), EBIT (earnings before interest and taxes) and EBITDA (earnings before interest, taxes, depreciation and amortisation). These measures are useful because if you are in control, you can change the level of debt, the charging of interest, your depreciation policies and your tax situation.

These measures may sound daunting, but they are basic common sense. They reflect different lines in a standard income statement, as shown in the simplified statement in table 20.1. The third column in table 20.1 shows the 'multiples'; that is, what each measure is multiplied by to give the valuation of $7 million. It is clear that multiples rise as you move down the income statement in order to value the business at the same level. This is not always the case. Depending on negotiations, the price of the business may be valued more aggressively based on the EBITDA line.

Table 20.1: sample simplified income statement

Operating revenue	$4 600 000	
Operating expenses	−2 850 000	
EBITDA	$1 750 000	$7m = 4 × EBITDA
Depreciation and amortisation	−450 000	
Operating income	$1 300 000	
Non-operating income	+50 000	
EBIT	$1 350 000	$7m = 5.2 × EBIT
Net interest expenses/income	−50 000	
EBT (pre-tax income)	$1 300 000	$7m = 5.4 × EBT
Tax	−300 000	
Net income or earnings	$1 000 000	$7m = 7 × earnings

EBITDA

From table 20.1, you can see that EBITDA is simply the income arising from the operations of the business; that is, operating revenue less operating expenses. It does not take into account depreciation charges (against your physical assets), amortisation (of your patents and intangibles) or any other expenses.

EBITDA is a very close approximation of operating cash flow. It is near the top of the income statement and shows your cash earnings before taking into account the cost of capital, tax or other variables further down the statement.

EBITDA is useful because it indicates how much debt a company can support. In this sense, it determines how much someone could pay for your business if they were to buy it with borrowed funds. It reflects the principle discussed in chapter 17: 'If you can't do it with someone else's money, it's probably not worth doing'.

Imagine an extreme illustration. Say the company in the income statement above has no debt and a private equity firm plans to buy it using funds borrowed at an interest rate of 10 per cent. On the basis of its EBITDA, the company could service a total debt of $17.5 million. That is, the company's EBITDA of $1.75 million is enough to pay interest on $17.5 million at 10 per cent. That figure is itself a valuation—one arrived at by estimating how much you could buy the firm for using borrowed funds.

This is the reasoning behind a leveraged buy-out (LBO). If the business is bought for $17.5 million, it could be leveraged with a $17.5 million loan. The focus on EBITDA is because the other costs further down the statement are not necessarily relevant to the decision. Depreciation and amortisation are not cash outlays, so do not affect the ability to service the debt. Tax is not an issue because interest payments are deductible.

Implications for management strategy

In reality, such a transaction would be subject to deeper analysis of the firm's potential as well as negotiations, but the example illustrates the basic principle behind the so-called LBO. It shows the power of EBITDA in deciding value. The challenge for the acquiring firm is to squeeze the operations and management of the business to grow the firm to a value greater than the purchase price. They would be likely to focus on working capital management, labour and other costs, in order to increase the EBITDA. These are the management strategies that invariably follow a private equity capital injection or acquisition.

Those in control of a business can then look further down the income statement for other options, such as selling non-core assets or outsourcing or leasing rather than buying. This raises non-operating cash to reduce borrowings.

EBIT

EBIT is earnings before interest and tax have been deducted. It is a more realistic statement of what the business can earn after it has accounted for the maintenance and replacement of its asset base. However, there remains the nagging issue of paying for any debt that the firm has to service.

Implications for management strategy

Focus on EBIT neglects the issue of interest expense, so you need to also assess how you are using your assets. If you have product or service lines that do not produce returns in excess of your cost of borrowing, you need to make strategic decisions on whether to reduce them, improve their return or replace them with different activities. It may well be that a particular line is a growth asset that is material to the firm's expansion and success. Nonetheless, a comparison of its cost and return — either now or in the future — needs to be part of your management thinking.

EBT

EBT (earnings before tax) is self-explanatory. It needs to be monitored because, via appropriate tax planning, you are in control of it and you can affect its value.

Net earnings

Lastly, we come to net earnings or income, which brings us back to where we started. This allows us to calculate the EPS and the P/E ratio, which values the business after all those other factors have been taken into account. For investors in the stock market, this is the bottom line.

Use the appropriate measures

This is not an exhaustive list of valuation measures. One alternative is to simply apply the NPV calculation discussed in chapter 18 by using the overall value of your firm as the initial cost of investing in it, then discounting the returns over a period of time. Used this way, the NPV is known as a 'discounted cash flow' (DCF) valuation.

The point of the chapter is to add perspective — to draw attention to the various angles that you and others should examine when setting a target for the potential value of your business, and to see how you can achieve that value.

21 Understand public funding
Work with the community

All public bodies—federal, state and local—have a vested interest in the success of the economy, the environment and the community in general. Arising from this is a wide array of funding opportunities that can bring together your business and the community it serves in a common purpose.

This is not about philanthropy. Public bodies rarely have all the resources to put public policy into action. They need to work with the business community to reach social objectives. See this as a partnership, not as a handout. Before you start looking at what is available, think about what your business does to contribute to the community's goals. Look beyond the obvious. Look to serve and assist. For example:

- Are your products useful to schools?
- Do they coincide with fulfilling national objectives?
- Do you provide services that are not reaching disadvantaged sectors of the community?
- Can you mobilise underused skills or resources within your region?
- Can your services assist attempts to reduce carbon imprints or contribute to other green initiatives?
- Can you provide assistance to a foreign aid project?
- Is there an international market you are not servicing but you feel you could penetrate if only you had some financial help?

Look for opportunities

If you type 'business grants' into your search engine, you will generate over a million hits. They will include:

⋙ *Export promotion.* Austrade will subsidise up to 50 per cent of your expenses in marketing your product in a new export market.

⋙ *Wages and labour.* Various programs will assist directly in the cost of employing new people; apprenticeship programs underwrite the hiring and training of new apprentices.

⋙ *Regional support.* Rural industries can receive direct grants to create jobs or to develop new businesses, including farms and associated activities; there are even payments to stay on a farm or move off it.

⋙ *Research.* The federal government and all states encourage research and development of new products and processes.

⋙ *Environmental projects.* There is support for product development and marketing, as well as subsidies for cutting energy costs through solar and other initiatives.

There is potential government funding in all of these areas and more. But don't approach it expecting a quick return.

Expect it to be a process

Anyone who has worked on a government tender will tell you that it is not wise to approach it as a means of quickly earning income. Rather, examine your own business strategy and that of the government and see where they coincide.

If you can see where there is potential for a legitimate partnership—that is, real mutual benefit—you will have a platform that is strong enough to handle what will at times be a frustrating process. It's a specialist area and if you don't have that congruence, the effort will be time-consuming and short on real results. That is why many corporations that undertake public works delegate the job to a specific division dedicated to working with the government. It is a business sector in its own right.

Do some research

You can obtain guidance on this from public bodies themselves. There are also consultancies that specialise in public tenders or in finding relevant grant opportunities.

Put aside an hour to look for opportunities that coincide with your business operations. Treat this as an opportunity to look at your firm from a different perspective. Be open to activities that you don't already do but have the resources and infrastructure to undertake as new business. Look for ideas that lead you to grow your firm to its absolute potential.

To begin this process, go to the grant finder at <www.business.gov.au>.

Rent or buy?

Assessing ownership

The value of your business premises moves with the property market. It is not just a matter of economic conditions. Property is a subsector of the economy. Real estate values can reflect supply and demand, changes in zoning, interest rates or issues specific to your location.

These values shift regardless of what is happening to your business in particular or the economy as a whole. At some stage, you will need to determine whether you are better off owning your premises, selling them or possibly leasing them out to move to a better location. There are numerous considerations in this decision, but the guiding commercial principle is how the net result compares with your cost of capital.

In earlier chapters you considered your own financial measures, such as the cost of capital. These measures set a hurdle rate that an investment—like buying your own premises—must return if it is to make financial sense to your business.

Put the decision in financial terms

The simplest calculation is the net yield on your property. Say you are paying $2750 per month in rent. The owner pays rates and property taxes, which amount to $4200 per year, but you pay all other outgoings. The owner wants to sell the property and is asking $450 000.

Your rent amounts to $33 000 per year. If you owned the property, you would also have to pay the rates and taxes; therefore, the savings you would make through ownership would fall by $4200 to $28 800.

Meanwhile, you estimate that transaction costs will add $12 500 to your purchase price, bringing your total outlay to $462 500. Your return on that outlay will therefore be 6.2 per cent ($28 800 divided by $462 500). This is the yield on the property.

How does this compare with your cost of capital?

The return may be lower than what you would earn by investing that amount in your business. But then maybe it should be. You can often secure cheaper financing if a loan is secured against physical property. Nor will you be faced with the uncertainty surrounding lease renewals. Property investment may be lower risk. And, as you are no doubt aware, forecasting the returns of your business can be a much riskier exercise than forecasting rental outgoings specified in your lease contract.

The simple alternative is to compare it with the cost of borrowing the money. If, say, you can secure the loan against the property and borrow forward at a fixed rate equal to or better than 6.2 per cent, it is a fairly neutral decision in financial terms. However, if your business offers substantially better returns, you would either not purchase the property or look for a better price.

Guidelines for pricing

To determine a prudent purchase price, reverse the yield equation and apply a 'capitalisation rate' or 'cap rate'. This is a rate that would be acceptable after considering your cost of borrowing. For example, if you feel that your cost of capital or the return you should generate on the property should be 8.5 per cent, capitalise your net rental savings at that rate.

In our example, if we wanted $28 800 to equal an 8.5 per cent return, the price of the property would need to be $338 823 ($28 800 divided by 8.5 per cent). The owner may not be willing to sell at this price, but you have now put some science in place to help you make the decision. You also have some logic to support your case during negotiation.

Other factors

Your decision needs to take account of various other factors, including tax. Although the outgoings (either rent or interest) are deductible expenses, the structuring of the transaction and how the asset is held needs to be assessed in the light of your overall tax planning. You could decide to have the company hold the asset, or it could be held by an independently incorporated entity. This is not a decision to be taken without the appropriate advice.

Food for thought

The McDonald's story remains instructive in the area of mixing ownership of premises with a tenanted business model. The original logic of the highly successful fast-food chain was to develop a standard business template that would rent out a real estate portfolio. Initially, the expansion and exploitation of the property holdings of the owner came first; the business implementation of the tenants came second. We all know the rest.

The point is to view your decision about premises in terms of the cost of money and the return you want to receive on your capital. The same logic applies to decisions to lease equipment or buy it.

Examine your business in these terms. Assess your financial structure. Are you using your capital to create the best returns? Do you have the right mix of ownership (equity) and debt?

The cost of borrowings will rise the more indebted you are, and there is a point at which this cost equals or passes the cost of using equity. In classical financial theory, the point where they are equal is where the mix is optimised.

23 Understand forecasts and analyses

If you don't know how to use a spreadsheet, learn now

In 1984, I was an eager young investment analyst in the research team of a Hong Kong stockbroking company. I spent my days working on large sheets of accounting paper ruled with lines and columns.

We would model quoted companies, try to work out exactly how they made their money, what their margins were, how their expense base was structured and what their likely prospects were. Some of these models were impressive in their depth and scope. Some would have to be laid out on drafting tables as we tinkered with the sheets of ruled paper that made up the model.

Then, of course, something would change. Hopefully it was near the bottom of the table, not the top. Because if it was up there—say some new process that radically altered the cost or function of one input at the operating level—we would have to amend every number all the way down through margins and operating income, through depreciation and amortisation, via volume numbers and sales forecasts, adjusting for interest payments and eventually tax before we came to the bottom line of net earnings. It was ultimately this number and its likely direction that would largely determine our view on the stock, and on which we would base various valuations (such as those outlined in chapter 20).

Then we would begin to examine 'what ifs'. It was a laborious exercise. It was the reason the models were always written in pencil and erasers were kept handy.

A life-changing experience

Then I went to a one-day course on the spreadsheet Lotus 123. My life changed that day. This was in the early days of PCs. Up to that point, I had always regarded PCs as glorified type-writers. In fact, they were still then known as word processors rather than computers. But now suddenly everything was possible. Within a few weeks I had transferred every model onto a spreadsheet. Every assumption was modelled under different scenarios. Calculations became mathematically more complicated and assumptions were tested to a deeper level. The process of investment analysis became dramatically more sophisticated overnight.

The speed of my response to changing circumstances was equally dramatic. I could point and click and there was the new earnings number. The same process could test the 'what ifs'. For investment analysts, this was a revolution. If you were born after 1970, you probably don't know it happened.

I am not even sure that Lotus 123 is still marketed. It was such a fundamental product that it was quickly developed by the software industry. Various spreadsheet programs (such as Excel) are now available, and the capabilities have hugely expanded. However, what amazes me today is that so many businesspeople—born before or after 1970—still keep their basic computer skills to a level capable only of receiving and sending emails.

Lift your analytical skills

This is not a call to dramatically confront your technophobia. Rather, it is a call to open your thinking to extremely simple analysis of the numbers that make your business tick. Spreadsheets are not computers. They are software. They are extremely simple to use. They are so much a part of modern business that they are always included in office software packages. Virtually every computer comes with them.

Start using them now. There are many services available within and outside your firm that can undertake highly sophisticated analysis of all aspects of your industry and your business. What you as a businessperson, manager or executive need to be able to do is test some of your own thinking—develop some of your own scenarios and see what impact they may have.

Every chapter in this section has worked through key business issues that can be analysed in detail by your accountant or finance director. But each of them also contains a kernel of thinking on a central issue that you, too, can simply model—no matter how primitively—on your own PC using a spreadsheet. As we have pointed out, all of them—cash flow analysis, capital management, valuation, financial measures and more—are very simple concepts. But they are concepts that management needs to fully understand. You should be aware of the opportunities they offer.

The quickest and most effective way to determine the impact of changes in these areas is to experiment with them on a spreadsheet. Then you will begin to fundamentally understand them. You will rapidly gain insight into what matters and what doesn't and, more particularly, into what actions will have the greatest impact on your business.

Don't delay

If you want to put the Pareto principle into some short-term action, sign up for a one-day course in spreadsheet applications now. If you already know how to use spreadsheets, sign up for the advanced version. This is an opportunity to seriously leverage your business acumen.

PART III

Recharge your team

Managing people is a daily task. For many, it is a daily challenge. In 'Recharge your team' you will look at how to form a cohesive group, no matter what its size or its purpose. The focus is on serving others. It's about assigning roles to the right people, maintaining their commitment, aligning them with the central mission and keeping them on track. You will also tackle the problems of performance appraisal, effective delegation and handling difficult people. A step-by-step guide will help you handle one of the hardest management tasks — letting people go.

24
Start serving
A holistic view of service

I once worked for a chef who ran a five-star restaurant in a ski resort. His passion was customer service. He demanded that staff focus entirely on the experience of our patrons. Unfortunately, he did so obsessively. When a waiter returned to the kitchen to refill an empty salt shaker, he would not acknowledge that she was attending to her duties. Instead, there was an explosion. He would scream at her, 'Why wasn't this already checked?!'

It was not unusual for our waiters to weep while serving.

Is a narrow service view effective?

Did this management style improve the customers' experience? The waiters still seemed to receive tips, but the chef never did. As a humble kitchen hand observing this from the dishwasher, I sensed a disconnection. While our chef would parade around the restaurant oozing charm and looking for compliments, our staff were deeply unhappy. And if a customer so much as suggested a minor thing was amiss, the head waiter would be publicly upbraided. It was not a pleasant experience for anyone.

'Anyone' included everyone who contributed to the process: our suppliers, who just didn't like dealing with him; the ski resort community; and managers of other businesses. Many of these people would have been occasional patrons of the restaurant.

Even students like me, who were doing a seasonal job to work on their skiing, were demotivated. We might have been part-timers, but the business couldn't run without us.

The restaurant was rarely full. It was only booked out when the whole valley was full. Staff turnover was massive and, predictably, there were cases of sabotage. An aggrieved staffer might turn the gas off at the main or leave the freezer off overnight. A waiter would simply walk out in the middle of a sitting.

It could all have been handled differently if the chef had broadened his service obsession to include serving his staff.

Why stop at customers?

Service has become central to management thinking. Marketing seminars, management theory, sales development and the like have focused on how to serve the firm's ultimate customers. That is a useful end in itself, but it too often defines the process as a one-way street—one in which only the customer is the beneficiary.

Service can be a productive force all the way up and down the food chain. It should be part of a firm's dealings with all stakeholders:

- ⇨ the shareholders, who provide the risk capital
- ⇨ the managers, who direct the business
- ⇨ the employees, who make it happen
- ⇨ the suppliers, who provide the inputs
- ⇨ the community in which the firm operates
- ⇨ the clients and customers, who purchase the outcome.

All of these stakeholders have needs. Fulfilling them has a broader impact, just as a rising tide raises all boats. Motorola, a company known for effective people management, acknowledges this in its internal slogan: 'There are people who serve customers, and there are people who serve people who serve customers'.

Reverse the conventional thinking that your staff are there to serve you or the firm. Look instead to how you or your firm can serve your staff. It may sound like a sentimental statement, but you will rise by lifting others. So will your business.

Begin with small actions

The salt shaker episode could have been managed differently. The chef could have organised a five-minute session with the wait staff to create a list of checks to be performed before each sitting. He could have delegated responsibility for it and then focused on the cooking.

My wife runs an equestrian business, breeding, boarding and training horses. Stable staff functions such as mucking out, grooming and cleaning are necessary and often tedious. Keeping good staff is at times problematic. But over time, she has assisted keen staff to take on more responsibility

One key member started as a part-time stablehand and has grown to become stable manager, releasing my wife from various responsibilities and adding status and motivation to her own job. This person's skill set has been enhanced with training encouraged and supported by my wife. The principle is to serve employees' needs to better themselves and their skill sets, rather than to improve the immediate prospects of the business—even if over the longer term that is the outcome.

You might think that this is basically just good management, yet it is surprising how little thought managers and business owners give to the personal development of their staff.

Put a service perspective on staff development

Elsewhere in this book we will look at business functions through the lens of serving the needs of the stakeholders involved. Because the internal economy of a business is a circular flow of relationships between all stakeholders, we can gain a new and powerful perspective by treating each of them as the start of the food chain rather than simply part of it.

Make a list of your key staff or your immediate reports. Think of them as customers and use the same guidelines you would use in strengthening customer relations:

⇢ *Focus on quality.* How will you make this a positive experience?

⇢ *Communicate.* Develop a two-way dialogue, not a one-way flow of words.

⇢ *Deliver.* If you promise to do something, follow it through.

⇢ *Prioritise.* Focus on developing a quality employee, not a product.

⇢ *Check your attitude.* Take a positive view of their talents.

Take note of their contributions. Don't limit this to their existing skill sets or functions. Take into account their more intangible strengths: their loyalty, enthusiasm, trustworthiness or positive attitude. Are they open to new ideas? Do they have abilities that are only used occasionally in their current function but could be used more in new areas of business? They may have particular advantages arising simply out of the generation they happen to belong to. Do they have strengths that offset other people's weaknesses? Does the list suggest a rotation of responsibilities?

Just making this list will generate ideas.

One small step

Identify someone on this list that you feel you can assist. Don't make this a massive task that you will regret taking on. In the words of Mother Theresa, 'If you can't feed one hundred, feed one'. It doesn't have to be the best performing staffer. It may be someone in whom you can see potential but who is currently not achieving it. The critical factor is how you can serve the employee.

Schedule a session with the employee. Explain that this is not a performance appraisal and communicate exactly what it is about that person that you really value. Acknowledge the contribution of the employee and if there is some small reward that you can offer, do so.

Ask the employee about his or her current role and personal development. Is there is any improvement that the employee would like to see in his or her position, skill set or level of responsibility? Ask how you could support this.

It may be that nothing will be apparent at this meeting. But ask the employee to think about it and come back to you with any ideas.

This a small first step in building trust and loyalty with your staff. You may well be surprised at the result.

Corporations increasingly look on personal career planning as a staff service run by human resources departments. It needn't be that formal or structured. What you have just done is take a first step in exactly the same process. Ultimately, it is a step towards team development and the powerful leverage of serving others. By helping someone climb a hill, you will be nearer the top yourself.

Work with others

I can't, we can

A surgeon can't operate without an anaesthetist and a nurse. A Formula One driver doesn't compete without a pit crew. Wherever you look, teamwork brings results. Bill Gates might be credited with starting Microsoft, but he did it with his partner, Paul Allen.

Gates may be a technical whiz. As chief software architect, he was key to Microsoft's product development. But the management team is headed by Steve Ballmer. He has been CEO for more than 10 years. Gates is still non-executive chairman, but it is more than seven years since his software responsibilities were taken up by Ray Ozzie and Craig Mundie. Microsoft is not the story of the Lone Ranger — and even in that enterprise it was his loyal companion, Tonto, who regularly saved the hero from a potentially career-ending scrap.

When investment guru Warren Buffett decided to give billions to charity, he had the Bill & Melinda Gates Foundation put the money to work. When asked why he didn't do it himself, Buffett simply said: 'I'm no good at that. The Gates Foundation is.' This is the same principle. A good team can achieve the result you want. It allows you to play to your strengths. Buffett's strengths lie in raising money in the first place.

Why do teams work?

All these examples make the same point: we can do things alone, but we do them better when we collaborate. What's more, it comes naturally to us if we let it. Two things make teams so effective. Both reflect our natural instincts.

1 *We like groups.* Virtually all living things form communities. Among natural instincts such as seeking food and shelter, there is the desire to form groups. Human beings are social animals. It is a survival mechanism. Our desire to work with others leads to a successful community—one in which all our needs are more easily met through collective action.

2 *We are all different.* A community includes a range of people with different capabilities. That means many skills are available to fill the various roles needed to make the community function effectively.

These two elements support each other: we are motivated by our desire to be involved, and our differences help us achieve our goals together. Working with teams builds on our natural condition. It leads to better ideas, and it leads to better execution by a group of people who are individually more fulfilled and motivated.

What makes a good team?

People often think a good team is one made up of heroes. Not necessarily. The key to making a team work is putting the right people in the right roles. They may not all be heroes, but they must be capable of fulfilling the roles they are given and they must be committed to doing them.

The right roles

Having the right roles is the crucial starting point. Consider this simple sporting analogy.

I can run. Not fast. But I can run. If I was part of a five-person team for a four-person relay, I'd be the reserve. If called, I'd do my best on the day. Our chances of winning would be slim, but my presence would ensure we participated in the race; we would have a chance. Other teams might have called on their reserves and it might turn out that I am the strongest reserve. Or things could change: someone could drop a baton, or a key player might have a bad start. We may place ahead of where we thought we would. We might progress to the semifinals when we thought we wouldn't make it through the heats.

By then, our best runner might be available again. I could drop out, knowing that my job was done. Although I was the slowest in the team, we would not have achieved what we did without my contribution. In short, I was given a role. I committed to it and carried it out.

So, even in our simple relay team, it all started with making sure we had the right roles for the job. In this case, we had a starter, two middle runners, a finisher and a reserve for backup. Collectively, there was a chance we could be heroes.

The right people

In addition to having the right roles, you have to have the right people for the job.

When developing a team, don't just look at the hard skill set; look at the strengths you need to achieve the desired goal. These strengths are often things that are hard to define, like analytical insight or marketing flair. And people often underestimate the importance of these strengths. They accept that they are naturally good at something, but assume that everyone else is too. The fact is they are not. Other people are good at something else. Most of us are capable of doing many things, but we are better at some than others. You need to align those natural strengths with the role.

In Rugby Union, everyone is playing the same game, yet there are two distinct types of players: forwards and backs. The role of the forwards is to compete for possession of the ball.

Once they have possession, they pass the ball to the backs, who hopefully will do something with it that will gain advantage.

The roles require completely different athletic skills and body shapes. Forwards are the ones 'without necks'. They have strong wrestling skills; their style of play is aggressive and determined. Backs are the lean ones who can run fast. Agility and spatial awareness are more important for them. Neither forwards nor backs are good at the others' jobs, but together they make a team.

How do teams work in business?

Individual effort can achieve a lot, but in business (as in sport), no single person has all the skills necessary to produce the ideal outcome. Working together can achieve great things; competing with each other may not. If you want to be slightly better, be competitive. However, if you want to be exponentially better, collaborate.

Again, it is not just about knowledge and qualifications. Personality types matter just as much. A team of analytical people may produce great analysis but not reach a conclusion. A group of highly organised individuals can work methodically towards a goal, but it may be the wrong one. Strategic thinkers might see the whole picture but not implement the strategy. Artistic people may make a product look terrific but can't sell it. Decisive leaders can make decisions, but they can't do all the other things. But putting these people together can achieve greatness.

Like any team, a business team will not work effectively without a coach. This is where you come in. Don't see this as a role reserved for senior management. It is required at all levels. You may be the divisional manager, the team leader, the founder, the entrepreneur or the small business owner. It doesn't matter. Even you and your assistant are a team. Team management skills are required at every level.

Start a team now

You don't need to wait for an opportunity to get a team moving. Opportunities can arise simply by starting a team. In fact, you might have already thought about some opportunities that could be taken up by a team.

Choose an area where you think your business, division, products, management or general services can be updated, improved, reduced, expanded or radically altered. It can be in any part of the business. It might be prompted by competitive advantages you already have, or by changing business conditions. Maybe there is a particularly talented group of employees that you think have potential for development. Ask them for ideas.

You could consider setting up teams to take on one or more of the following tasks:

↠ Rebuild the company website.
↠ Develop a new service or product.
↠ Expand into a new market segment.
↠ Introduce just-in-time inventory management.
↠ Start a new internal training program.
↠ Review your supplier relationships.
↠ Change the management structure and reporting lines.
↠ Apply new technologies.
↠ Develop a new credit policy and implement it.

No business is too small or too large to use its teams effectively. The efficiency of a small retail outlet can dramatically improve if you simply draw on the personal strengths of just one or two members of the counter staff.

Use this exercise to focus on something that you intuitively know needs to be done—something that will make a difference. Do not be afraid of the potential for change. The process will be motivating and uplifting for you and your team members.

Take the following steps now:

1 Define the area you want to examine.
2 Outline the reasons why you want make changes.
3 List the strengths and weaknesses of the existing situation.
4 List the skills and responsibilities required to produce the desired outcome.
5 Choose the people you want to attend the first meeting of the team. In doing this, you may be faced with some difficult decisions. There may be personnel who might be offended by their exclusion. This in itself is not sufficient reason to include them. Let the objective be the determining factor. Both the objective and the team may change after the first meeting, but to begin, choose those who are required and are capable of contributing.
6 Get started. Let the participants know what the meeting is about and ask them to come prepared with ideas. You have already done enough preparation. The way to progress will emerge as the process unfolds. In chapter 26 you will look at the next step.

26
Develop a motivated team
Target your strengths

The aim of the first team meeting is straightforward: discover and define an achievable objective that draws on your team's strengths.

Start with the positives

Begin with a simple SWOT analysis. You are already familiar with the process because you did a personal version in chapter 4. Remember, the analysis is not an end in itself. It's simply an organising matrix that focuses on what is the best course of action with the resources available. It also has the advantage of being extremely easy to implement.

Make sure you appoint a team member as official minute-taker. Much of this process is best managed around flip charts or a whiteboard. A lot of ideas will be suggested, but you will need to maintain a written record of key developments.

Strengths

Begin examining the issue the team will address. Starting with strengths, ask these questions:

- ▷ Where are we now? What is already working?
- ▷ What strengths do we have as individuals?
- ▷ What strengths do we have as a team?

Brainstorm this. Momentum will build during the process. If at first you feel stuck, look at your strongest suit in the area you are discussing: where is your product or service or organisation working well? Don't forget that even if it isn't working particularly well, that may turn up later as an opportunity. For now, focus on the positive.

Spend time on this. Be exhaustive and be open to anything. Individual strengths that seem irrelevant may in fact open up new ideas. For example, theatrical talents may well prompt exciting presentation opportunities. The hobby of one member may lead to a lateral marketing initiative. The fact that you are in business at all means that something is happening somewhere. This in itself is a strength. How can you build on it?

Start with strengths because this is necessarily a positive action. Don't stop this process until you feel you have covered the area thoroughly.

Weaknesses

When you move on to weaknesses, there will be a mine of information. Don't hold back on pointing out shortcomings. Addressing them may provide your biggest leap forward. Equally, they can guide your actions away from areas where you lack strength and where your efforts would be wasted.

Opportunities

By this point, some opportunities may have already emerged. Your strengths will suggest areas where you are very capable. They may already be working well. Examine whether even greater emphasis on them can give you even more competitive advantage. Are there weaknesses that can be easily reversed through minor product changes, new skills training or new staff?

Threats

Threats are usually in areas external to the organisation and are often matters over which you have no control. They include things such as new directions in public policy, major shifts in economic conditions, changes in market demographics, and the introduction of new technology that may change the landscape in a way that is not yet apparent. Nonetheless, threats may also camouflage some opportunities. Don't exclude any.

Narrow down the opportunities

Isolating the best way forward can only be done when you have exhausted all scenarios. You may not follow through on every opportunity, but you will now have a list from which you can choose. By eliminating the least-preferred options, you can start to focus on exactly where it is you want to go.

Distilling some action from the process is the most important step. However, this is the first meeting, so don't expect definitive strategies straight away. Instead, identify the opportunities that have emerged. Go through them one by one, assessing each on its merits and targeting your best ideas. Try to limit the number. One is often the most effective.

Be specific

Clearly identify the opportunity. If you are going to put a team process in place, what is its objective? Work with the team to imagine what the result would be. Develop specific goals that define a successful outcome.

You may find that the team wants to run ahead of this process. Ideas on what needs to be done, who will do it and when it should be done will creep into the discussion. This is a good sign of enthusiasm, but those questions are better left to a structured meeting that specifically addresses them. That is the agenda for the next meeting.

What you need from today is a tight definition of the objective. Conclude the meeting with a clear statement of what it is. A successful objective will have five characteristics. It should:

1 have a sense of urgency (is important to do *now*)
2 be compelling (*needs* to be done)
3 generate commitment (have team members who *want* to do it)
4 align with the goals of the business (be part of the *overall* plan)
5 be realistic (*can* be achieved).

The last step is to set a date for the next session. That meeting will be about how you are going to reach the objective: how the group is to be structured, who will have which responsibilities and what the timeline is going to be.

Structure a functional team
Roles, goals and leadership

'We must all hang together, or assuredly we shall all hang separately.' So said Benjamin Franklin at the signing of the American Declaration of Independence. It was a call for cohesion and unity at a time when there was little of either. Although the ensuing war led to a victory for US independence, a common purpose was slow to build. And that's the point. It has to be built.

Achieving anything with a group of people requires organisation. A team can only be cohesive and unified if it has an intelligent structure—one in which roles are clearly defined so that, collectively, they achieve a common purpose. In short, you need to align roles with goals.

How do you begin?

Develop roles with reference to the agreed objective and the route the team will take to achieve this. The initial part of this process is to set out the path the project will take and then to break it down into the tasks that have to be undertaken at each step along the way.

Examining a critical path on a step-by-step basis reduces any project, large or small, to a sequence of achievable elements. The ultimate objective may appear quite grand, possibly even overwhelming, but if you break it down into small steps you can take each one at a pace that suits the team's capabilities. The plan becomes a series of small tasks to be completed in a certain sequence.

Start this process by reviewing the team's objective. Know exactly where you want to be and what it will look like when you arrive there. Then, leave the outcome to one side and go back to the beginning. What is the first step you have to take to go in that direction? You should never lose sight of the objective, but its achievement requires you to focus on the 'here and now'. What do you need to do now to begin the process?

Create a road map

Preparing this pathway is a creative exercise that draws on the collective talents of the team. Allow this discussion to encompass all the issues that arise. The solutions to many problems that could appear along the way may be evident at this early point. Although the pathway is still in the planning stages, some wrong turns can already be eliminated. When you have completed this process, you will have a list of the tasks required for a successful outcome. You will have a road map in the form of a comprehensive and logical list of what has to be done, and when.

Allocate the tasks

Only when this list is complete is it time to assign roles and responsibilities to each of the team members. Remember that this is a team. You may be the boss, but in this process you are also a team member. Discuss the roles collaboratively; do not simply assign them. Focus on the strengths that individual members bring to the assignment. Allow all members to acknowledge their own abilities, and equally, to make it clear where they might not be suited to a particular task, or where they or the team think they will need assistance.

Figure 27.1 provides a template for developing and recording roles. Give a copy to each member. Work through it methodically to achieve the result you want from this step.

Figure 27.1: a tool for role specification

Role specification—Team member
Name:
Title:
Key role:
Strengths:
Existing skills:
Strongest contributions to team goals:
Personal targets:
Skill development:
Resources required:
Key actions:
Timeline:
Performance parameters:

You want a cohesive team in which each member has clearly defined responsibilities.

Consider each element carefully. Discussion of each will generate greater buy-in on the project, together with mutual understanding of the responsibilities of each member. This will build empathy and cooperation. Remember these guidelines:

- *Titles matter.* They need to be accurate and acceptable to the team as well as the individual.
- *The key role is an expansion of the title.* A person may have broader responsibilities within the team. Some teams are sponsored by a senior manager, a board director or an external mentor. If so, specify what is expected of them. If there is a team leader, define that role. If that person is you, don't limit the conversation to your ideas. Ask the team to assess your strengths and your potential input. Ask them what they see as your contribution. How do they think you can help them? What do they expect from you?
- *Acknowledge the strengths of each member.* A team built around roles that draw on strengths will be far more effective than one that attempts to accommodate people's weaknesses. Make sure the right person is in the right role. Shuffle responsibilities according to people's capabilities.
- *Review existing skills.* This process is not to focus on shortcomings but to make sure the team is aware of the entire skill set available. Also, people are often competent in areas that are not immediately relevant to the task but may be useful in the future.
- *Agree on the strongest contribution that each member will make.* This is important. It can be a simple mission statement for each individual member. It should be honest, and it should inspire them. It needs to be respected and supported by the team as a whole.

▷ *Identify real individual targets.* This is more tangible. The targets are specific. They relate to actions that are to be completed comprehensively and on time.

▷ *Identify any further development or training needs.* If the project requires a specific skill that is missing from the team, examine adding the right person. If it is appropriate to train a team member, assign the role to the member with the appropriate strengths to optimise the training.

▷ *Check that you are properly resourced.* This may include physical assets, people, premises or space. However, it may also mean responsibility or status in certain areas so that people can not only make decisions but also implement them.

▷ *Summarise the key actions.* These are things that are critical to the mission.

▷ *Develop a realistic timeline for completion of tasks.* Note those tasks that are co-dependant on the completion of other members' tasks.

▷ *List performance parameters.* These will allow members to assess their own progress, and ultimately their overall success, in achieving the outcome. They are not the basis of an appraisal system. Rather, they are agreed criteria that can be useful along the way. Often, they are simply a means of regaining focus.

The result

When you have completed this, the team will have a clear structure. All members will know exactly what is expected of them. By including the whole team in developing it, you have brought together a collaborative group—one that is cohesive and unified. It will achieve the objective by hanging together.

28

Manage the team

A good sailing breeze often comes with rough seas

Much has been written about the performance of teams: why they work and why they sometimes don't. Personalities do matter. They can have both positive and negative effects on the outcome. Much of the negative energy can be eliminated by the work you did in chapter 27. By clearly defining the roles, you effectively introduced boundaries that, if adhered to, can limit the opportunities for friction to arise.

Nonetheless, don't expect teamwork to always be smooth sailing. Being aware of some key theories about group work will help you stay objective in difficult times. It is not the intention of this book to examine these theories in detail, but a knowledge of some will help you to observe team dynamics rather than be overwhelmed by them.

Tuckman's stages

Among the more famous theories is Bruce Tuckman's 'forming', 'storming', 'norming' and 'performing'. There have been various adaptations of these ideas since he developed them in the 1960s. The essential elements, however, remain evident in the evolution of most teams, be they business, social or sporting ones. Be prepared to experience the characteristics of each stage.

Forming

In this stage, the territory is as yet unknown. The group is just coming together, getting to know each other and assessing the lay of the land. Be prepared to lead by example as to the sort of behaviour and input that is required.

Storming

This is often a rocky period as members demonstrate aspects of their personalities, form bonds with other members and assess how they can align their actions with their responsibilities. Prepare to be tolerant of both the process and the behaviours, but it may be up to you to ensure that behaviour is appropriate and cooperative. Again, lead by example when the opportunity arises.

Norming

The team is now starting to gel. Members have adjusted to one anothers' styles, working relationships are starting to develop and a sense of progress is emerging. Try to avoid any regression to the storming stage. Focus on the progress made and the maintenance of it.

Performing

This is where the team is working as a cohesive entity. A key feature is interdependence. Problems are solved collaboratively. New ideas are accepted and analysed with positive energy. The group starts to display the characteristics of a winning team.

Observe the stages

Teams can move in and out of these stages at different times, especially when members or management change. And the same team may not always work as well when charged with a different function. That may require a different team altogether.

I see this in both nature and business. In one particular business it is very apparent. My wife and I breed horses for both fun and profit. It's a commercial operation that is also central to our lifestyle.

In managing large numbers of horses, we are regularly required to have in the same paddock animals with quite different characteristics. The results can be fascinating. Half a dozen horses in a field develop a hierarchy of roles reflecting their psychological and instinctual needs. There are nurturers, loners, gluttons, young ones, mothers, fathers and pregnant broodmares, just to name a few. Collectively, though, those roles shuffle into a natural order; one that serves the cohesiveness of the herd, just as would happen in the wild. In doing so, they go through a very similar process to the one just outlined as the group develops into a performing team.

Manage the natural order; don't fight it

The objectives of horse breeding and development require a controlled mix. For example, you would not place a precocious stallion in a herd of mares that are in season unless you want a certain result. Similarly, you might try to curb the excessive behaviour of young colts by exposing them to the quiet presence of an older broodmare. So, deciding who should (or should not) be on your team is crucial to achieving your outcome.

When you put a new horse into a paddock with an established group of horses, you will see them go through the same process again, as they first form, occasionally storm, start to norm and eventually perform as part of the team. There are times, though, when it simply doesn't work. For some reason, the collective psychology just doesn't gel. In those cases, which are rare, we simply change the mix.

This is not a lot different from human behaviour. Be aware as you manage your group that this is a normal procedure — one that you need to monitor, assist and occasionally guide. Avoid buying into the emotions or issues that may arise.

My experience is that if the team is properly structured and collaboratively developed, the results will be uplifting and rewarding. But if it's clearly not working, you may need to do the human equivalent of changing the configuration of the herd and shift one or more members to a more appropriate paddock.

Maintain performance

It's about what's going right, not what's going wrong

Thankfully, there were no appraisal sessions when I worked in the ski resort restaurant (see chapter 24). If there had been, my own goal for the session would have been to get out alive. Contrary to the chef's approach, appraising someone's performance is a service. It is a dialogue in which the interests of the employee have equal weight with the interests of the business. If there is to be any bias, it would be to err on the side of the employee. Balance may be best, but often it cannot be established without ensuring the employee's position is soundly based — that there is a steady platform on which to base a real discussion. People need to feel open, not threatened.

Should you appraise performance?

Performance appraisal does not have a great record. Some studies show that it can curb performance rather than enhance it. Control groups free from such practices regularly outperform those who are subject to it. There is often a fear around appraisal for the employee, while the person charged with carrying it out is often untrained, finding it little more than a time-consuming irritation. So, should you do it?

If you feel that these sentiments apply to you, and you have no training in appraisal, the answer is 'Probably not'. If appraisal is handled badly, it is likely to increase stresses for the employees and work against your relationships with your immediate reports rather than enhance them.

Positive appraisal

The opposite view is this: a positive and functional approach to appraisal can grow stronger employees, boost cooperation and develop loyalty. If you want to put this sort of relationship in place, you will need to approach the task with a mirror image of classical appraisal techniques. Reverse some of the ingrained emotions you have around the process and focus on personal development rather than performance appraisal.

Performance management expert Robert Bacal feels that many appraisal programs fail because they focus on the wrong things:

> They focus on appraisal *rather than* planning. They focus on a one-way flow of words *rather than* dialogue. They focus on required forms *rather than* communication. They focus on blaming *rather than* solving problems. They focus on the past *rather than the* present *or the* future.

This is a very neat summary of the attitudes you need to shift if you are going to manage performance in a way that is a positive experience.

The power of listening

Many people struggle with listening. It has never been one of my strong suits. For a long time, I took the view that only the person doing the talking was actually doing anything; that the listener was some passive entity who was not really doing much. Nothing could be further from the truth. It is impossible to have a conversation without having both a talker *and* a listener. It's a 50:50 arrangement. That is what a conversation is: a dialogue between two or more people, not a one-way flow of words.

To improve my listening skills, I have often forced myself to play the role of the listener. It doesn't come naturally. I have to remind myself ahead of entering some conversations that receiving information is equally as powerful as giving it. The results are often astounding. I have had consulting sessions where I confined my input to asking questions, then simply listened to the answers. An answer often raised the next question.

The outcome has been invariably positive. If we were focusing on a particular issue, the other party could work out for themselves exactly what solution was required. And they are far more inspired and motivated by a conclusion they have arrived at themselves than by one suggested by me. I sometimes look back on these situations and think I really didn't do much. But I did. I listened. We wouldn't have achieved our goal if I hadn't.

This is what communication means. One problem with appraisal techniques is that they tend to follow a formula. The human resources department or the textbook has produced a form that must be followed, regardless of the needs of the individual in question. Some kind of record-keeping is required, but a motivational result is more likely to come from free-flowing communication than from filling out a standard form.

Look for solutions, not problems

An appraisal meeting often starts by focusing on a problem. No-one in the process is going to feel particularly comfortable with this. The employee may be fearful or angry about it; the manager may feel discomfort in addressing it.

The way out of this is to focus on the solution. Do not ask not what the problem is; ask what outcome would resolve the issue. Ask for their *solution*, not yours. Ask questions and build the discussion around that. A solutions focus generates positive thinking. A problem focus breeds blame and negativity. Neither party could be expected to enjoy this experience, let alone produce a good outcome.

Think about now

Focus on now. That's the only time you can do anything about anything. Examining future possibilities may help you plan, but the outcome of your dialogue needs to be about action you can take now. Generating an action that can be implemented immediately can turn a feared appraisal into a positive step forward.

Some simple guidelines for an appraisal dialogue

If you feel that you and your team can benefit from a session based on these sorts of principles, try it out. You may choose to work with only one person to begin with. You don't need to put together a highly complicated format, but it will help if you plan the session. A rough structure will put some order into the meeting and the record you keep of it. The following guidelines will help you begin:

1   *Limit the number of people you appraise.* You can start with one. I always recommend keeping the number to a minimum for several reasons. An overly long list simply becomes a burden. You cannot really provide support to a large number of people. In a corporate situation, you may struggle to get this down to a manageable number like five or six, but try to keep it in single digits. If yours is a small and busy business, choose one or two of your key or influential employees. In a broader management role, confine this to your immediate reports, and leave them to do theirs. This is the sort of delegation you should be putting in place, and you can lead by example — put in place positive principles that they can follow. When you decide who to support, identify those who you really think you can help, or those who may need help. Be aware that there may be some people who will respond better to someone other than you.

2   *Always take notes.* There is nothing worse than entering
    a later session with no memory of the style, content and
    outcomes of the previous one. Keep these in a single
    book or file for easy reference. Periodically, you may
    want to remind yourself of the issues facing a particular
    individual or what actions you have decided to put in
    place. Refer to these occasionally if you are practising
    'management by walking around'. People are motivated
    by knowing that other people know, understand and care
    about their position.

3   *Start the session positively.* Talk about the things that
    are going right. This is easy with a high performer;
    it can be more difficult but is essential for someone
    who is struggling. If an employee is scoring four out
    of ten, something has helped achieve that four. What
    is it? Simply turning up on time? If so, acknowledge
    this punctuality. Looking at what someone does well
    indentifies strengths. Help the person appreciate his or
    her own abilities. Make a note of them as well as any
    achievements.

4   *Ask about the person's role.* Have the person list the key
    tasks he or she is charged with and together work out a
    short job description stating what these responsibilities
    are. This is effectively a statement of the person's role.

5   *Ask what the person thinks about his or her performance.*
    Are there areas the person would like to improve? If so,
    choose an area that is already satisfactory (or better) and
    ask how the person might apply that experience to lifting
    performance in another area. Would assistance or further
    training in specific areas be helpful? Are the right resources
    available? Is the person well supported by colleagues?

6   *Specify an action.* You now have a description of the
    person's job role, a list of areas where some changes
    might be possible and an understanding of what sort of
    support is needed to put them in place. Together, decide

on a specific action in one or more of these areas. Don't go overboard. Make it an achievable action that can be done in a certain time. Develop a plan to put it in place. Most importantly, identify the first step, however simple, that can be taken immediately.

7 *Note the proposed action.* Thank the employee for his or her input and say how you look forward to seeing progress. Make it clear that you are available to reassess the person's situation and development at any time. Set a time for a review, but don't make it too soon. Sometimes once a year is enough. Other situations require a quarterly session, or more frequent review. Just don't commit so much of your time that it becomes a burden to either of you.

This is not a tight formula. It is open to wide-ranging discussion, but it does help you initiate action. Over time, a career development plan will emerge for the person in question. Let it evolve. Some people will respond better than others. Many will be pleased to have some focus on their efforts. They will look forward to building their position in the firm through an ongoing dialogue managed by sound principles.

30

Decide who will do it

Management is delegation

You have probably come across people like Tim. He was my colleague for 15 years. He was the guy with the clean desk.

Our business was based in Hong Kong and had a dozen offices spread around the region. We were a successful firm and were constantly in a growth phase. There was always something going on. We enjoyed buoyant economic and financial conditions. Asia was on a roll. We were not without regular crises, but somehow we seemed to handle them.

That was all very exciting, but it meant juggling a lot of different jobs or projects, be it opening another new office somewhere in the region, introducing a new marketing product, or simply changing roles within the organisation. As a result, my office was usually a mess.

Tim's office never was.

I was astounded by this tidiness. The in-tray was clear. The diary was on the desk—closed, not open. Tim's single notebook sat beside the empty in-tray. For someone like me, who had an office littered with an intriguing array of in-trays and must-do piles, this didn't seem right. I knew Tim managed a lot of things very well. I just couldn't see the evidence.

Tim was ruthlessly productive. Things were done the way they should be done, by the people who should do them, and by the time they should be done. I asked the simple question: 'How do you do it?'

His answer was: 'When a piece of paper lands in my in-tray, I pick it up and ask myself, "Who is the best person to handle this piece of paper?"'

Management. It's that simple. The evidence of Tim's managerial productivity was staring me in the face. It was his uncluttered office.

Find the time

Delegation is the essential art of managing. In fact, you could argue that the ultimate manager never actually does anything else. The manager simply organises everyone else to implement the vision. There is a lot to be said for this. If you are wondering how you will find time to manage, the answer is this: find the time to delegate.

Think about consequences

People who don't delegate effectively will invariably spend too much time doing the things they are weak at—and it takes a lot longer to do a mediocre job of something you're not good at than it does to do an excellent job of something that uses your strengths. Do you want to be someone who does a lot of mediocre jobs, or do you want to be someone who does a lot of excellent ones?

Failure to delegate is expensive. If you decide to do too much by yourself, it is likely that you will:

ᐅ lose the respect of your colleagues, because nothing will be done on time
ᐅ fail to develop the capabilities of your team and your colleagues
ᐅ find you simply do not have the time to do what is actually your job
ᐅ spend very little time doing the things you are good at
ᐅ become overwhelmed with stress and frustration
ᐅ be overtaken on the management ladder
ᐅ lose your confidence, and potentially your job.

Delegate!

So, if you are holding that piece of paper in your hand, ask yourself two questions:

1 Am I the best person to handle this item?
2 Is managing this item myself the best use of my time?

If the answer to either of the questions is 'No', ask yourself a third question:

3 Who is the best person to handle this?

Working out the answer to this question will lead you to examine the skill levels of your colleagues and the capability of the firm. The best person may not even be in the firm. The best 'person' might be a supplier, an acquaintance, a service, a consultant, a friend, a relative, a firm that specialises in outsourcing that particular task, or someone you haven't yet hired. The most important thing now, however, is to find out who the best person is and to delegate the task.

There is a tendency to think of delegation only in terms of major projects, but even if you are giving that piece of paper to your personal assistant to file, that is delegation. It meets all the criteria for successful delegation:

- ☒ You have nominated *who* is the best person to do it: your assistant.
- ☒ You have explained *what* it is you want done: have the paper filed.
- ☒ You have made it clear *why*: you have decided to have a clear desk.
- ☒ You have nominated *when*: now.

This is no different from what is required to delegate the most complicated task. You may need to take time to choose *who* is the right person. Maybe a team will be required, as well as a team leader. Exactly *what needs* to be done may need closer examination and team discussion, as may *why* and *when*. But if you focus on being very clear on each of the *w*'s, you will have exercised very precisely the most powerful skill in the executive toolbox.

There are a number of popular management acronyms you can use to help you in this process. SMART is probably most in vogue. It suggests that the task you are delegating should be:

‣ *specific* — very clearly defined
‣ *measurable* — able to be monitored and assessed
‣ *agreed* — all parties must be willing to participate
‣ *realistic* — actually achievable
‣ *timebound* — having specific starting and finishing dates.

This is a useful acronym, but in the interest of simplicity and speed, use the four *w*'s for now. Try it. Think of an item and run through the steps in table 30.1.

Table 30.1: steps in delegation

Task	Define the task; give it a sensible title; check that it's SMART.
Who	Who is the best person or team to manage this? Do they have the right skills? Is more training required? Does that fit with their level of responsibility? Does it stretch them? Will it encourage or challenge them? Are they in need of, or capable of, 'stretching'?
What	Precisely what needs to be done? Are there established ways of doing this? Be very clear about how you want this done. Spell it out. What are the criteria for the assignment's success?
Why	What's important about this? How is it good for the firm or the team? Why have you chosen them? Let them know. What's in it for them? How will it help you? Remember that effective delegation contributes to the business while giving the employee both recognition and motivation.
When	Make sure there is a deadline. Explain why. How will delivery be monitored? Make note of a time to check on the task's progress. Agree on completion dates. Be clear that it is okay to ask for help.

Some things to remember

One thing to remember about delegation is this: no-one does everything the same way as anyone else, including you. If what you want done is a process and it must be done in a certain way, give extremely clear instructions.

If, on the other hand, you are more concerned with the result than the process, give the employee or team some breathing space. Let them apply their own creativity to the task. By all means, intervene if it is clear they are heading for disaster. But, within reason, let them find out things for themselves. You might be surprised when they deliver a result that exceeds your expectations.

Properly executed, delegation can play a key part in determining what your human resources policy should be, who you should be hiring, how you are monitoring your business, what measures you incorporate into performance appraisal systems and how you motivate those around you.

For individual managers, delegation is a means of handling tasks in which they do not excel. There is no shame in this. Glory for you lies in applying your strengths. You might be an excellent football player, but on Thursdays it's cricket and at best you can bat in the middle order. You might wonder: 'Why, then, am I captain?' It's because someone saw your strengths and promoted you. It is impossible to have a cricket team without a middle order. Your skill set is essential to the task at hand. So are your leadership strengths. Delegate the job of opening the batting to the best people for the job. Revel in their success. Thank them publicly for their efforts. They may never be captains, but then those who open the batting rarely are.

But when it's time for football, don't hold back. Go ahead and shine.

Handle difficult employees

What to do when it is not working

Standout employees are almost defined by the lack of management attention they require. They tend to be self-starters. They have identifiable strengths that suit their role. They respond well to new ideas and suggestions, often seizing on them to take things forward.

Core employees may need more guidance but, properly managed, they do the job and are part of a functional team.

Difficult employees are much harder to deal with. They take up a disproportionate amount of management time. They can have a negative influence on team performance and in many cases they are immune to attempts to improve the situation.

One problem in such cases can be management itself. No-one really wants to confront the situation. There are niggling issues for which no resolution seems apparent. Management is often slow to react, allowing the situation to fester and the politics around it to become more complicated—often to the point that doing something about it will only create more problems.

In most jurisdictions, there are clear-cut rules for dismissible offences. But these are often the obvious areas: theft, violence, drug and alcohol abuse, bullying and the like. Much more challenging are people who are simply 'difficult'. They may be chronically late and defensive about it. They may disrupt team efforts. They may indulge in excessive politics. They may be rude and aggressive, or passive and non-compliant.

You have to take action

There is a line in most organisations beyond which certain behaviour is not only unacceptable but also downright destructive. The good news is that as owner, or manager, or team leader, you will intuitively know where this line is. The bad news is twofold. It is up to you to do something about the unacceptable behaviour, no matter how uncomfortable it feels. Also, you have the difficult task of objectively defining what the problem is.

When you become aware of unacceptable or destructive behaviour, you must act. Failure to do so will be costly. Respect for you as a manager will be diminished, co-workers will feel demotivated, and performance will suffer. You may have procrastinated on this already, but you need to stop ignoring it now and confront the issue. What will you do?

Make a calm assessment

First, set aside some quiet, uninterrupted time to assess exactly what the behaviour is. Think of concrete examples of where the employee's actions have caused a problem, and in each case define:

1   the action
2   the impact.

For example, if the person is chronically late, note:

1   exact instances
2   the impact (for instance, it makes it impossible to demand that co-workers be on time when someone is chronically late without penalty).

If the person is discourteous to customers, specify:

1   an example
2   how the business is penalised through loss of customer loyalty.

If the person is rude and aggressive with colleagues:

1 write down an example
2 outline the impact this has on the morale and performance of co-workers.

If the person fails to complete certain tasks:

1 list them
2 describe the impact on operations.

Do this process calmly. You need to put a dispassionate platform underneath your assessment of the situation. Often it is hard to describe events objectively. Try the 'video' approach. Imagine a sample situation was filmed, then replayed without sound. The person in question walks into a room and does or says something that prompts a reaction. You do not hear what is said by any party, so you don't pick up on any of the verbalised emotions. Just silently watch the interaction and write down what you saw happen. Apply this to a few different situations and you will start to generate a clear statement of what is not working. Make it a statement of fact, not emotion. Write it down in the action/impact format: 'When you ..., the impact is ....'

When you have done that, specify the management issue that arises from the behaviour. That is what you are responsible for. For example, being rude to customers (the action) loses business (the impact). The resulting issue for which you are responsible is the maintenance of customer loyalty. That is what you have to manage. It is your job and it is a fact. Stick to that fact. This is a commercial situation. You are not meant to be a counsellor or a therapist. You have to take action to maintain customer loyalty.

Follow a process

Arrange a suitable time for a session with the employee and let him or her know that you want to discuss a management issue. There is no foolproof formula for this meeting, but

I have found that the following format produces positive results:

1 *Stay calm.* Immediately prior to the meeting, make an undertaking to yourself that you will remain calm and stick to the facts.
2 *State your role.* Open the meeting by acknowledging your own part in it. Make the point that as a manager, you have a responsibility to ensure the smooth working of the business. Use the 'issue' part of your statement as an example of your responsibilities (for example, maintaining customer loyalty or encouraging punctuality). Then clearly state the issue: 'When you ..., the effect is ...'.
3 *Ask for input.* For example, you could say: 'I have to manage this. What do you think I should do about it?' This may prompt a wider discussion about the situation. Don't be tempted to judge this conversation or the actions of the employee. Just listen. Prompt the person with questions. Ask for ideas that might be a solution. Your action/impact/issue statement outlines the facts. Stick to them, and regardless of where the conversation goes, stick to the fact that this is a problem. It has to be managed and that is your job. Feelings, either yours or the employee's, need not enter into it.
4 *Take a break.* It may be that the discussion becomes difficult or reaches an obvious stalemate. Call time out if it is clearly going nowhere, but in doing so, restate that you have to manage the issue. An agreement or action that resolves it must be made by a certain time. If a short-term bandaid solution emerges, don't reject it out of hand. It may provide the basis for further consideration during a cooling-down period. But stay firm that the underlying issue must be addressed, and will be, by a fixed date.

5 *Be objective*. Handle the situation gently and dispassionately; then it is likely that a solution will be worked out. Even difficult people can see reasons why the manager has to manage. They will see why you have to address the issue and how its resolution will be beneficial to the business. Their problem is often the difficulty they find in maintaining their intentions. The discussion may also have raised areas where you may need to act to support the solution. This may be anything from speaking to other employees to lifting the skill set of the person in question. You therefore need to work out what actions will be taken, and by whom, and ensure that these can be written down and agreed upon by all parties.

6 *Apply a timeline*. Set a date when the situation will be reviewed, and be clear that any lapses in the interim will bring the issue back into immediate focus. You may choose to make this a formal, verbal warning. If you think it is necessary, make this clear to the employee and make a precise note of it.

7 *Close on a positive note*. Thank the employee for the effort he or she has put into discussing the issue and say that you are looking forward to managing it in the way you have agreed. As always, let the employee know you are available to discuss this, or any related issues, if they arise.

What is a 'good' result?

If you are lucky, this process will have a beneficial effect on the person concerned and the functioning of the business. That has been my experience. But there are no guarantees with 'difficult' people. They may have deeper issues, but you are a manager, not a counsellor. While compassion for personal problems is essential, you are not equipped or qualified to handle them.

Going there is dangerous for them and for you. If it seems that outside support would be useful, suggest it, and be prepared to support it if they are prepared to make the effort.

By carrying out this process, you have started to manage the issue. Be aware that the discussion itself is progress for you and for the employee. You have probably bonded with the person a little and you now understand them better. That is a good thing, but don't let it blind you to any subtle re-emergence of the issue.

It may turn out that some people are completely inflexible, or that their performance is subject to chronic lapses in behaviour. However, by carrying out the process outlined, you have provided an opportunity. They may choose not to take it and you will have to choose your next step. Nonetheless, having established a dialogue, you will find future sessions on the subject will be easier, not harder. The issue is now clear.

Let people go
How to do it properly

It is rare to get through a business career without having to dismiss someone at some stage. Neither party enjoys it. Yet you have a responsibility to handle it.

There are two reasons for this. The first is that your firm and your co-workers deserve a cohesive and productive work environment. It is a management responsibility to provide this. Letting someone go may well be a constructive act in making this so. The second is that you, or your firm, hired this person in the first place. You may have made a mistake, or the person may have changed in the course of this employment, or conditions surrounding the person's life and work may have shifted. It doesn't really matter. It is up to you to handle it correctly. Not doing so will affect your ability to manage others, and, increasingly, incorrect handling will expose you and your firm to legal liabilities.

Be respectful

It is very important that you honour both parties. The departing employee needs to be left with his or her dignity intact. This person now has to manage a major life change and needs as strong a platform as possible on which to do so.

Just as importantly, you need to honour yourself. If, in the process of letting someone go, you avoid the key issues, employ dishonest spin to soften the blow to both of you, or buy into the employee's grievances at the expense of others' reputations, you will not walk away with a sound belief in yourself. You need to know that you have handled this with integrity.

Always check the legal position

In most jurisdictions, the process of dismissal is now broadly regulated. Australian workplace legislation, for example, determines the rights of both employees and employers in most situations. It is essential that you are fully aware of these regulations. They cover various issues, including matters of bias and discrimination, but also areas where immediate dismissal is warranted.

For small to medium-sized enterprises, there are various relaxations of the rules that apply to large corporations. These concessions are hardly generous to small business, but they do acknowledge the lack of specialist human relations resources, the impact of time lost on small operations and the lack of flexibility in assigning an employee to another task.

Employers' responsibilities vary from state to state. There is no excuse for not knowing these rules, and you should be able to access them easily. They are usually well spelt out on various government websites and are easily located by your search engine.

In addition, some of your employees may be subject to specific contractual arrangements with the firm. Whatever the case, the starting point prior to considering any dismissal needs to be a full understanding of your legal obligations.

It happens

We are assuming in this chapter that you have reached a point where dismissal is the only option. You may have applied techniques outlined in earlier chapters on handling difficult people or managing performance, but they haven't produced a positive result. It is likely there has been at least a verbal warning and a written warning and that you have given the employee the opportunity to address the issues. In any case, this is often demanded by the relevant legislation. You have also looked at alternatives and have finally made the decision that there are none. So how do you go about it?

Some guidelines for dismissal

1   *Be prepared.* Prepare the case for dismissal objectively and methodically. Refer to the action/impact/issue model in chapter 31; that is, the person in question has acted in a certain way and this has led to a certain impact in the workplace. In turn, that has raised a management issue, which it is your job to handle. Events have been such that the only course left is to remove the action that causes the impact. In this case, it means letting the person go.

2   *Be honest.* You can acknowledge the person's strengths, but in this case they do not outweigh the problem. In fact, a change of employment may enable the person to employ those strengths more productively in a different environment. I have let go people who have gone on to be extremely successful in other organisations, or in their own business. None have come back to thank me, but they have handled the dismissal constructively, and so have I.

3   *Investigate options.* If you think there is a case for it, examine the outplacement opportunities. You may know of alternative employers that could actually use the person's talents or style. It may be that the person would develop more positively by undertaking certain training or retraining. If it is within your power or budget, offer to assist with this. Such an offer is not required by law, but it will serve your firm well if you are able to serve the outgoing employee in a clear, positive and dispassionate fashion.

4 *Maintain privacy*. Have the dismissal meeting face-to-face in a private space. You may choose to have a second person to act as a witness or a steadying influence. If you have a human resources department, an experienced person should join you to explain any queries regarding the firm's termination policies. Nonetheless, the dismissal should never be conducted publicly.

5 *Stick to the facts*. Make it clear as soon as possible that the decision has been made. There is no backtracking. This is not a negotiation. Don't apologise. You are not making a mistake. You are managing the situation. By all means be compassionate, and be prepared for emotional displays, be they anger, frustration, sadness or tears. Listen to them and acknowledge their fears and concerns, but do not let the interview drag on. Instead, after a suitable amount of time, move on to the firm's policies on departing staff and the employee's termination entitlements and explain what's next.

6 *Choose the time*. Many people suggest rules about timing. Some say the meeting should be on a Friday. Others say being left to stew all weekend is not a good result, so recommend a Monday. Every manager and employee is different. Take advice and assess the appropriate action. Generally, though, it is not a good idea to have an employee on the premises after the decision has been made.

Follow-up

Just as important as the above is what you do after. Here is a checklist:

1 Document the process and the outcome clearly, objectively and precisely. This is to cover your legal responsibilities but also for reference in handling similar events in the future.

2   Ensure that all the employee's entitlements and rights are implemented immediately and in full.

3   If required, call a team meeting to explain what has happened and why, especially if the person has been a disruptive influence. Keep this dispassionate and constructive. It's about going forward.

4   If the departing employee was responsible for relationships with certain clients or customers, contact them immediately. Explain your actions. There is no need to go into detail, but they need to know how their account will be treated in the future.

5   Review your own performance throughout this process with a view to how you will handle such matters going forward, whether they be at the hiring stage, the firing stage or the people management in between.

Accept this change

Letting people go is part and parcel of the evolution of any business. If, after due consideration, it is the only option available in the circumstances, act promptly and manage it as the right and proper thing to do, not the wrong thing to do. If it is carried out fairly and reasonably, both parties will benefit, as will the reputation of your firm.

PART IV

Recharge your firm

What can you do *now*? 'Recharge your firm' doesn't develop long-term plans; it explores what you can do in the present. You will identify exactly where you stand in relation to your stakeholders. Treating your business as an ecosystem will generate innovative ways of recharging your business. You will analyse your market position in terms of competitive edge, internal strengths and where you and your products stand in the life cycle of your business. This will clarify your options for growth and profitability, such as buying new teams, merging with others, acquiring competitors or, for that matter, being acquired.

33 Manage your business ecology

Everyone has a stake in it

Think of your business as an ecosystem. Just as the environment depends on the interaction of different entities to survive and flourish, so does your firm. When all parts of your environment are functioning smoothly, so does your business. Equally, the failure or dysfunction of any one entity can affect the sustainability of the whole system. It's a two-way street.

In the natural environment, those entities are known as species. In business, we call them stakeholders. Examining their needs will reveal all sorts of opportunities to optimise your enterprise. It's not a matter of generosity. There is an essential ecology to your business. If you want a sustainable enterprise, you need to optimise the environment in which it operates.

Healthy relationships

Who are these stakeholders? We touched on them in the holistic view we took of the firm in chapter 24. Six groups have an interest in the success of any enterprise. They are managers, shareholders, employees, suppliers, customers and the community. If the environmental analogy doesn't work for you, think of these stakeholders as spokes in a bicycle wheel. If one is weak, the wheel will wobble. You will have to pedal harder, and your speed will be slower.

This is common sense. If you don't support your suppliers, your deliveries are unlikely to get priority. If you let workplace relations deteriorate, productivity will fall and staff turnover will rise. Ignore your community and you may be ignoring your customers. Lose sight of your shareholders' interests and they may not be there next time you need to raise funds.

But there is more to it than simply getting by. What would happen if you really tried to optimise the relationships between your firm and each stakeholder? Wouldn't you end up with an ecosystem that is doing more than merely ticking over? Wouldn't you grow an enterprise that is not just successful but highly motivated and profitable on a sustainable basis — a standout in your sector. We have seen how many natural species thrive when conditions are right. What can you do about your business conditions?

Biodiversity in business

Environmental science teaches us about biodiversity. Inject dysfunctional elements into an ecosystem and a species breaks down. Cane toads have shown us that it doesn't end there. The impact is broader. There is a chain reaction. Eventually the system itself can crash.

The business equivalent is a toxic culture. Its dysfunction is made worse when the focus is on the needs of only one stake-holder. It doesn't matter whether this stakeholder is inside or outside the firm. Internally, a culture of disharmony can be the undoing of the best-intended business. Externally, poor relationships with shareholders, your community or your customers can do irreparable harm. Serving the stakeholder universe requires a 360 degree view, as shown in figure 33.1 (overleaf).

When asked about external stakeholders, most people only mention the obvious ones: customers. Sometimes customers become the only focus, at the expense of workplace morale, financial viability or productivity; deterioration in any of these can lead to business failure. Or people overlook other key players, such as the suppliers and the community. Yet these two have come to play a crucial role in modern business.

Figure 33.1: six key enterprise stakeholders

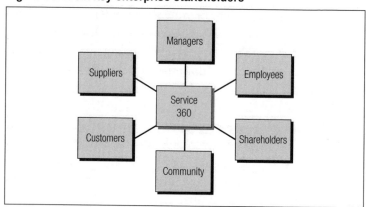

Build a cohesive culture

Take a new perspective on this. Review your business practices on the basis of how each stakeholder is being served. By putting the emphasis on how to *serve*, rather than how to *be served*, you can develop a new system for taking action. You will start to comprehend what each stakeholder requires to support their role in the enterprise.

Use table 33.1 to rate the quality of the relationships among your various stakeholders. This can be applied to any business. Go through each stakeholder in turn. From their point of view, what could you do to serve them better? Think about the guidelines in the following paragraphs.

Shareholders

You may be the only shareholder. In that case, what kind of service do you want from your business? You are already paid a salary to manage the business, but what do you want from your investment?

If you are part of a large, publicly listed corporation, your shareholders probably want a rising share price and/or a good dividend. But maybe they also want to be able to see for themselves how you are trying to achieve the mission; perhaps they want more transparency and better information.

Table 33.1: rating stakeholder relationships

Stakeholder	Relationship (1 = poor, 10 = excellent)	How can they be served?
Shareholders		
Suppliers		
Employees		
Customers		
Community		
Management		

Suppliers

Your suppliers may be better served by advance information on your production needs; this will help them deliver your orders on time. Are there opportunities where serving your suppliers can spur on business growth through jointly developing a new service?

Employees

We have already examined ways in which you can serve your employees. Try to think of someone, or some group of employees, whom you could assist by extending support in a specific area.

Customers

Customers' needs are not just the focus of the marketing department. Cross-fertilise. Try working with your suppliers to find better ways to service your market. Include employees with non-marketing functions in brainstorming new customer service ideas.

Community

A strong community awareness reflects well on a business, either on the national stage or the local one. Customers may choose to shop at Bunnings rather than a competing outlet partly because of their community activities. I have spoken to their staff about this. They decide which project to support not on the basis of generating business, but on the basis on what best serves the community's needs. Remember the Chicago gangster, John Dillinger? When asked why he robbed banks, he said, 'Because that's where the money is'. For Bunnings, the community is where the business is. It is where the customers come from.

Management: what about you?

That leaves management. It sounds like you are doing all the serving. How can you be supported?

Have you actually asked anyone this? It takes a confident and dignified manager to ask employees how they can help. Yet subordinates will usually respond very positively to requests for support. It might require genuine humility for the boss to say, 'I am struggling with this. Do any of you have some ideas that will help me with it?' Remember, you will often find that those around you can be your strongest mentors.

Work together

Don't limit this analysis to what you alone can do. In your next team or management meeting, raise the notion of the circular flow of stakeholders and ask members to rate the different relationships. Then examine how each of them might serve a stakeholder better to lift the ranking of each relationship. Better still, set up a think tank that includes a representative of each stakeholder.

34

Work with suppliers
The start of the food chain

In chapter 33, you examined the relationships between stakeholders in a broad sense. What happens if you investigate this further? If you take a closer look at how you can serve some of those relationships, what business opportunities arise?

Start with those most often overlooked: your suppliers. Almost by definition they are assumed to be at the bottom of the food chain. If you are not being properly served by your suppliers, there is something wrong with them. Right?

Alternatively, your perspective could be the problem. Try thinking about your suppliers as being not so much the *bottom* of the food chain, but the *beginning* of it. If you are not satisfied with their service, have you actually told them? Have you looked at anything you can do to make it better?

Serve the servers

You touched on this in chapter 13 when looking at Toyota's pioneering role in just-in-time inventory management. By sharing production plans with suppliers, Toyota could take delivery of components only as needed, thereby cutting inventory expenses and reducing the cost of capital. Suppliers could plan their production levels to more efficiently meet the changing or cyclical needs of the customer. They managed their own business better as a result. This collaboration led to research and development partnerships in which the suppliers developed new products that helped their own businesses as much as Toyota.

So the policy had mutual benefits. It underlined the reality that suppliers are not there to be beaten up. They may be there to serve, but they serve best when they themselves are served.

Constant evolution

Not only the Toyotas of this world benefit from this perspective. A colleague gave me this example. A small firm began by collecting empty toner cartridges for a cartridge refilling company. The service was appreciated by high-volume cartridge users, as the environmentally friendly disposal requirements were cumbersome and time-consuming.

The firm collected them for free, stored them in a central warehouse (a garage) and sold them to the refiller. Business grew to the point where collection was outsourced to an external operator. The firm designed a branded, purpose-built container for empty cartridges that stowed easily in the transport firm's vehicles. The transport firm handled the job more efficiently as a result.

Eventually, the firm dispensed with the warehouse and had the containers delivered directly to the refiller. Freed from logistics, they moved into telephone marketing of the pick-up service, enhancing it by providing a turnkey offering — refilled cartridges were sold back to the customer at a price significantly lower than the cost of new ones.

The refiller thus became the firm's supplier but enjoyed higher volume. The transport firm developed a more extensive pick-up route through the city, adding value and volume to its business. All gained an advantage, including the environment.

The rate of such business evolution has increased with recent developments in technology. The internet has boosted the use of network partners, and many new businesses thrive on it. Obvious examples are software firms that develop programs to work on other people's operating systems. (Note the 'app' that appears on so many programs.)

In this environment, the mindset of being in combat with your suppliers is fading. It needs to be replaced with recognition of the ecology of a firm's relationships. The advantages to be gained from effective supply-chain management will come from working together—the focus needs to be on supplier relationships rather than just supply.

Shifting attitudes

This shift in attitude is often a big ask for established businesses, big or small. Supply is often considered a dull area—one in which the uninspiring task of the procurement officer is to constantly squeeze supplier margins in order to cut costs. There is nothing wrong with the goal of reducing expenses. The real opportunity, however, is to create new areas of value for both parties. It makes sense to serve the supplier in reaching their own goals, one of which is to serve you, the customer. Can you assist by offering training in relevant skills, or by seconding technical staff, or by direct financial assistance or investment? These are things that eventually boost the service that you receive. Many of them lead to lower costs.

If you are going to align your supply services with the organisation's broader goals (such as quality of product or service, reliable delivery and product innovation), the participation of all stakeholders will help. Dialogue between the firm and the supplier will improve if production, marketing and sales functions are brought into the loop. They too have a vested interest in the development of this relationship and can bring fresh ideas. So, of course, do customers. The focus is on how to leverage the firm's collective resources to not only fulfil but surpass the market's expectations.

There are at least five areas in which this sort of perspective can lead to management and market efficiencies. These are shown in figure 34.1 (overleaf).

Figure 34.1: benefits of serving suppliers

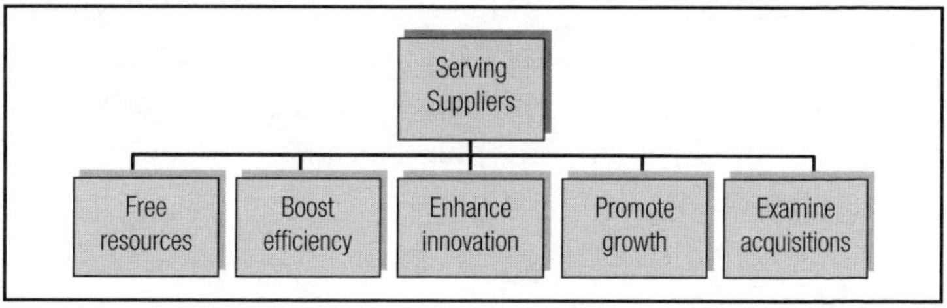

Free resources to focus on your strengths

In the case of Toyota, serving was the provision of information. The manufacturer shared its materials requirement planning (MRP) and its relevant forecast with the supplier. This is a powerful service. It helped the supplier avoid the waste of overproduction, yet it also helped them ensure they could produce enough for Toyota on time. That freed up their resources (in this case, capital), which in turn lowered costs.

Similarly, the design of a bin to hold empty cartridges took into account the ability of the delivery driver to lift it, move it and easily fit it in the vehicle. This allowed a quicker pick-up and ultimately a direct service from customer to customer. The small firm eventually disposed of its own vehicles and concentrated its resources on its main strength, which was marketing.

This illustrates a core feature of the network economy—the ability of a business to use alliances to free key resources. It enables the business to focus on its strengths. What tasks are holding you back from focusing on yours?

Boost efficiency

Supply-chain management has achieved great success in reducing lead times—not only in the delivery of a component or product to customers, but also in developing a new product and taking it from concept to market. The advantages are obvious. Shorter lead times in developing new products can lower costs and improve time-to-market. Delivering directly to customers cuts warehousing costs, enhances customer satisfaction and increases repeat business.

Enhance innovation

The supply chain is a source of new product ideas. Suppliers are often the first to spot trends. After all, they know what your competition is ordering. What additional services or product derivatives is your supplier capable of delivering? How can you take advantage of them? Or, as is increasingly the case in the network economy, what suppliers are offering a new product or service that you could easily integrate into your business? Can you work with them?

Promote growth

There is an insurance aspect to all this. It doesn't take a major financial crisis such as the recent recession to bring about difficult trading conditions. Your firm can be affected by plenty of other unforeseen circumstances, ranging from the collapse of a key customer, debtor defaults, input shortages or commodity price fluctuations, right through to industrial accidents, inclement weather and death or illness of key personnel. Assisting your suppliers in difficult times will benefit everyone. A firm can often accommodate a supplier's short-term financial difficulties by working out a discounted pricing structure.

Even when there are no pressing issues, it can be in both parties' interests to assist the health of the supplier's cash flow by prompt payment, or payment in advance, for specified lines of product or service. These arrangements are not just a means of squeezing discounts out of supplier prices; they can build trust and cooperation and open up opportunities for growth and product development. They can certainly improve your ranking among the supplier's customers.

Examine acquisitions

The relationship with a supplier only exists because both parties are part of the same economy. Vertical integration is hardly a popular business strategy, but ownership or integration of various stages of the production cycle can lead to a stronger market position, a better return on capital and the potential for economies of scale. Thinking about an acquisition may not lead to merger, joint venture, marketing alliance or acquisition, but examining the prospect will reveal where the relationship can work better for both parties.

Begin working with suppliers

Investing in a supplier could allow your firm to diversify into a new business area. But, equally, it could involve something quite simple, such as organising for your part-time bookkeeper to develop his or her skills in some new business software. This could cost you less than hiring a new employee, lead to a vastly improved service and grow the bookkeeper's business at the same time.

Supply-chain management also helps you focus on the sort of suppliers you want to deal with. Do they have the level of service and quality that your business demands? Are there too many of them? Would it be more appropriate to concentrate on key existing or potential suppliers who will benefit most from an alliance with your business?

Serve the owners
First in, last out

Shareholders invariably come last. This might sound contrary to the opening chapter of this book, or the opposite of what most company chairs say at AGMs. Yet the reality is that when the going gets tough, the shareholders are last in line.

Legally, that is certainly the case. When a business is liquidated, the first to be served are the secured creditors. If there is anything of value the liquidator can convert to money, access to those funds is first given to lenders who have charges over the assets of the company. Next are the employees, whose rights and interests are generally protected by law. The extent of that protection differs between jurisdictions, but employees are well ahead of the shareholders. So are all the other creditors who are owed money for products provided and services rendered.

In fact, when a liquidator compiles the list of creditors — that is, the people or institutions who will take a portion of what is left of the company — the shareholders do not even figure. If there is anything left at the end of the wind-up, they will have some value attributed to their shareholding. This is the ultimate risk that investors take when they buy shares in any business, quoted or otherwise. So it is not unreasonable that we take their interests into account when making business decisions.

The shareholders' perspective

In chapter 1, you learned that serving the interests of shareholders is the primary aim of any business. That, after all, is the mission. There is no other reason to start a business. That might sound unfashionable, but really there is no other reason. At the bottom line, shareholders are the ones taking the risks. As stakeholders, that's their contribution.

This does not mean a business can't have a moral stance, or can't adapt to shifting social needs or environmental concerns. It can make all sorts of decisions in those areas in the process of serving all stakeholders' interests. But a business has no interest in going broke. It can achieve nothing if it does.

The emergence of 'green' investment funds makes this point clearly. These institutions target their portfolios at companies that create environmentally friendly products and processes. Nobody puts money into these funds to lose it. They want a return, but they want to generate that return by supporting businesses that are aligned with their own preferences. The mission is still to make it work. No-one wins if the fund collapses.

There are a couple of other issues to address. Serving shareholders' interests is not socially divisive. In the decades since compulsory superannuation was introduced in Australia, this process has become more inclusive. The welfare of virtually every member of every family is now exposed to business performance via a shareholding in one form or another. One view is that this has co-opted the population into mindlessly supporting big business. An alternative take is that we are all in this together, so let's make it work.

Nor is serving shareholders' interests a divisive business strategy. The simple fact is that a business has to make a profit and it has to survive. Otherwise, all stakeholders suffer. The employees are out of jobs; suppliers have to cut back; the community has less service; management has nothing to manage; prices rise through less competition; and, ultimately, the shareholders will have no money to invest to make things better. When this happens in large numbers of businesses, it is called a recession. In very large numbers, it is a depression.

Creative engagement

So if shareholders are stakeholders we need to serve, how do we engage with them?

Start with the simplest case. You may think that these issues don't concern you because your firm is small, unlisted and has very few shareholders. In fact, you might be the only one. And that is exactly the point: what do you want?

Sole proprietors often just focus on managing their businesses. They see their enterprises primarily as sources of income or salary, boosted by occasional bonuses in the form of profit share.

This is not surprising if you fit in this category of ownership. After all, you may be the owner, but effectively, you are also an employee. But if you are only earning a salary, there is no point in owning the business as well. You might just as well see if you can earn more working for someone else and be able to enjoy your weekends. This is often the case with franchisees. They see the purchase of a franchise as buying a job. That happens, but there is no point doing it if all you end up with is a salary and a lot of stress. You need to be getting a salary *and* a return on your capital.

So what do you really want as a shareholder? The primary reason for investing in anything is to create wealth. You have to manage your business on a day-to-day basis, and you are paid for that. But what are you really doing to create value? Why do you own it? If you were to look at how this business fits into your life, what value would you put on it? If someone were to come along and offer to buy it from you at a price that made you think it was worthwhile selling, what would that price be?

Think about that for a moment and be realistic. What's the number? It is probably more than you think someone would pay, but what if you made it your target, so that in, say, five years' time, your business would be saleable at that price? That would be a shareholder's objective worth striving for. That would be a mission. Isn't the simplest strategy to make that the goal and then start looking at what you can do to make that achievable? You can pay yourself a salary along the way, but that's not really the point, is it? The goal is how much value you can create.

Clarify the mission

Taking this objective as your mission immediately simplifies a lot of your decisions. Think, for example, of your dividend policy. Exactly what amount of profit needs to be reinvested in the firm for you to reach your target? You could put all the profit in your pocket, but what else could you do with it? What is your growth strategy? Does is fit with the risk profile or time horizon of you, the shareholder? For example, would organic growth or acquisition help you achieve your goal sooner and with less risk? Should you focus on quality standards or quantity targets?

The same questions apply equally to large corporations. Reviewing your business with a clear mission in mind helps you to abandon ineffective practices; it also prevents internal processes building a life of their own.

A high-profile example of this is the business model of a New York investment bank. In the sub-prime debacle and its aftermath, it became clear that the internal compensation structures within these institutions had taken on a life of their own. Even in the middle of the crisis, several of these banks paid out more in bonuses than they did in dividends, and yet, at the same time, they required taxpayer funding to avoid collapse. There would be a great deal more clarity around internal compensation structures if they were rated by their contribution to the shareholders' mission.

These principles apply to all firms, not just large corporations. If you have more than one shareholder, there is a range of opportunities for collaborative action—you just need to approach the relationship from the point of serving your shareholders' needs.

Financial support

Funding is fundamental to the shareholders' role. If you are examining a new initiative, check it against the mission. Does it move you closer to those goals? If so, would it not be a service to your shareholders to let them participate directly in it? If your bank is prepared to lend you funds to undertake a project, they must have seen it as an acceptable risk. Why not offer the lending opportunity to your shareholders? You may be able to structure the facility such that the cost of capital to the business is less than what the bank would charge, but the interest payable to the shareholders is greater than the return they would earn elsewhere for the equivalent risk.

This is the principle behind a whole raft of fundraising options in the listed sector, such as rights issues, dividend reinvestment plans or offers of convertible bonds. The principle applies just the same in the unlisted sector. A shareholder loan is often the most cost-effective and uncomplicated way of raising cash, and one in which all can see clearly how shareholders' objectives and management strategy coincide.

Collaboration with shareholders should be embraced, not avoided. Even on a personal level, shareholders can provide advice and guidance. The mentoring and consulting role need not be confined to managers or directors. Can you draw on the expertise among your shareholders to maximise the skills and knowledge on which the management or your firm is based?

Take the shareholders' view

Taking the perspective of shareholders, then, can prompt alternative strategies for managing and growing any business, even in the case where the only shareholder is you. Run through the following checklist and see if the points suggest simple actions you can take via serving and collaborating with your shareholders:

▷ Target value creation — what do shareholders want your business to be worth, and by when?
▷ Seek guidance from shareholders to develop goals.
▷ Make shareholders' objectives the mission of the business.
▷ Analyse your strategy and decision making in terms of fulfilling that mission.
▷ Incorporate those goals in choosing the measures by which you assess performance.
▷ Add a shareholder(s) to your think tank.
▷ Examine alternatives for shareholder funding.
▷ Seek mentoring and consultation with your shareholders.
▷ Align growth strategies with shareholders' interests.
▷ Reassess entrenched internal structures and processes in terms of achieving the mission.
▷ Broaden your shareholder base. Investigate employee share plans.

Buy new business lines

Diversify or grow through acquisition

Does it make sense to grow your business by buying another one?

There are three good reasons why growth by acquisition can be much more attractive than expanding organically:

1 The risk can be lower.
2 Access to finance can be easier.
3 Growth can be faster.

Does that mean you should jump into the deep end of the acquisition pool right away? Probably not. Note that in those three reasons, we said *can* be rather than *will* be. Look at each one individually.

Lower risk

There is an inherent risk in any growth strategy. The addition of a new product line, entry into a new market or diversification into a new sector all come at a cost. Estimating the costs is not the hard part. Most businesspeople are able to assemble the required resources in the right structure to support an expansion plan. Costing these is a straightforward exercise. The pricing of the inputs, labour and physical assets is readily apparent and, in most cases, the business is already experienced in managing and accounting for these issues.

The problem with forecasts

Forecasting the return, however, leads the process into completely uncharted territory. I don't think I have ever seen a business plan that, when executed, has generated cash flow that exactly matches its forecasts. It is wonderful if cash flow exceeds the forecast. That's called success. But the point is, the firm underestimated the return. They may have done so for prudence and risk management, but nonetheless, the forecast was inaccurate.

The risk that a revenue forecast is wrong is so great that it is the core issue in determining whether or not to proceed with any plan to grow your business, organically or otherwise. Contrary to popular belief, growth by acquisition can often prove to be the less risky road to take. This is because an existing business can clearly demonstrate its business model and how it works. At its simplest, it produces A at cost B, then sells C of them at price D to produce revenue E for profit F. If a business is already doing what your expansion plan requires, much of the guesswork is taken out of the equation.

You may well say that an acquisition will cost more than organic growth, but that is precisely because the risk in the forecasting has been greatly diminished. Successfully executing an acquisition and efficiently merging it with your business will still be challenging, but many of the unknowns at the planning stage have been eliminated.

Easier financing

Because the forecast returns are based on already tested assumptions, financing for an acquisition can often be put in place quite easily. Banks, as we know, hate risk. Asking a bank to underwrite an untested business plan or a new initiative is like pulling teeth. They will either reject it outright, or provide you with only modest financing, or demand crippling security and charge interest and repayment terms that put the business under intense pressure. That is because they are acutely aware that forecasts are usually wrong.

Do not expect a much better response from venture capitalists. While they will be prepared to take much greater risk, it will only be at the expense of the ownership and control of your business. Deals funded by private equity invariably come with extensive caveats, rights to exit and obligations on the original owners that can create huge burdens. Their goal over a certain period is a profitable exit; it may be one you don't want to take.

Financiers prefer the known

Your ability to negotiate with either banks or other investors is significantly enhanced in the case of a sensible acquisition. The fact that you are taking over an operating business with known capabilities and an established financial track record seriously reduces the risk of the investment. As a result, financiers are more prepared to back the project and their demands will be softened by the extent to which the risk is reduced.

In the unlisted sector in particular, a new source of finance is introduced through acquisition: vendor financing. In a carefully and agreeably negotiated sale, vendors will often accept a purchase plan that can be accommodated by the cash flows of both the existing and the acquired businesses. Also, the interest rate for such a plan is likely to be lower than those in current financial markets. Putting together a mutually acceptable buy-out plan is often at the centre of a successful acquisition, and this can be a win for buyer and seller.

When an acquisition is fully investigated, the forecast outcome is more robust and the decision to proceed comes down not to the viability of the business you are buying, but to the price you are prepared to pay for it. This is a far more commercial decision, and one you can take using your own, known valuation measures rather than forecasts based on a greater number of unknowns.

Faster growth

Growth by acquisition is faster than organic growth. Implementing a new strategy to, say, double your sales over two years brings with it a raft of actions that will take time to implement. It may include gearing up production, hiring new staff, relaunching the marketing effort or developing new distribution channels. If an established alternative exists, taking it over will likely be a much faster route to your goal.

Why some acquisitions don't work

Although an acquisition strategy may look attractive, there remains the risk that it will not work. Many don't. The reasons for failure are varied, but fall into three clear categories:

1 It was an inappropriate target.
2 The acquirer failed to carry out exhaustive due diligence.
3 The acquirer paid way too much.

Start by looking at you, not them

Before you identify an appropriate target, examine your own business. What does it need? What does it do? How much can it afford?

Take a 360 degree view of your existing business landscape. Consider your stakeholders. Is there is a business case for merging with, aligning with or taking over a supplier? Or a distributor? Look outside as well. Include your competitors but also wild cards in unrelated businesses. Include all these as you review your options.

A checklist for acquisitions

You may already have organic expansion plans in place, but as an exercise, spend 30 minutes considering acquisition as a real possibility. Think about your space, your competitors and your future as you run through the following checklist:

1   *Capacity.* Are you fully using your production capacity? Can you produce more than you currently sell? Could a business with a new or similar product line add to your market coverage and at the same time use your spare capacity at only a marginal increase in costs?

2   *Sales growth.* Does a potential target embrace a customer base outside your current sector? If you are examining an organic plan to compete in that sector, work out the cost of adding each customer, then compare that cost with the cost of purchasing that number of customers through acquisition. How much would you have to pay?

3   *Geography.* This is an obvious one, perhaps, but markets often have location-specific characteristics and it can be less risky to enter those markets through an established operation. Where there is a clear boundary, there is also less chance of cannibalising your own business. Where is the nearest, clearly identifiable market that you are not addressing simply because of your location?

4   *Cross-selling.* What other products do your customers buy? If you are already servicing the customer, what else can you sell to them? Can you broaden the range of products you market with only modest expansion of your existing marketing efforts?

5   *Market position.* Can an acquisition increase your market clout? Would greater volume give you not only more control over your pricing, but also lower costs by commanding higher volume discounts on inputs?

6   *Strong teams.* Are you aware of management, sales or production teams in other businesses with particular strengths that your operation lacks? Hiring people and

managing staff is central to success but also problematic. Is there an opportunity to buy the configuration you want?

7   *Distribution.* What channels are you prevented from using or unable to enter with your current structure? What is out there that could seriously expand your market opportunities?

8   *Vertical integration.* Is there commercial sense in buying into either your customers or your suppliers? This is not just a matter of securing sources of supply or tying up sales. Does the space they are in have a stronger outlook than your own? Are you better off investing in their business rather than your own?

9   *Horizontal integration.* Are there existing businesses that you are confident you have the abilities and the resources to manage successfully, even though they are outside your sector? General Electric went from producing turbines to leasing them to being a global financial powerhouse. But it doesn't have to be that sequential. Are there growth businesses in unrelated areas that you could add value to?

10 *Competition.* Is there simply the opportunity to eliminate competition in your market sector, be it by locality, category or market segment?

11 *Similarities.* Are there businesses whose culture, style and product are natural fits with yours? A merger would simply boost turnover on a consolidated cost basis and open up opportunities in new markets.

This process alone will clarify the issues facing your firm and where it stands in the structure of your industry. It may well be that it reinforces your commitment to growing your business with its own resources. If it does prompt ideas that you think are worth pursuing, you are ready to move on to the next step: analysing and executing the opportunity.

Assess your acquisition

Due diligence

Don't do this alone. Think team. Working with a team is central to identifying and executing an acquisition. It doesn't need to be a large team. The smaller the number, the more focused it can be—and the less likely it will be to have confidentiality problems, especially at this early stage. A team will see more appropriate targets and identify more bumps in the road than you will. If you don't have the team in your firm, discuss your options with a mentor or two; or, alternatively, employ a trusted consultant.

Remember the alternatives

In chapter 36 we offered a list of areas to consider when thinking about acquisition. It is essential to build on the characteristics of your business, even if the target is external to the space you currently occupy. Does the strategy provide an opportunity to apply your strengths, address your weakness or contain potential threats? It must be a leveraging process if it is to produce an exponential result. This may not be just in terms of revenue. It may also be a defensive means of consolidating market strength, or a way to provide a platform for future growth.

To stand in its own right, an acquisition needs to meet the criteria outlined in chapter 36. Compared with organic growth, it must:

1   be lower risk
2   be more easily financed
3   provide results sooner.

Keep these in mind. It may well turn out that growing through your own resources is the preferred option. However, you will come to that decision via a rigorous route. Your understanding and implementation of an organic strategy will be better for having analysed an acquisition. One benefit of carrying out due diligence on an acquisition is that it stress-tests the organic alternatives. Try not to lose sight of this. Expanding via acquisition is often an exciting project, one that develops its own emotional momentum. But it is only a means to an end, not an end in itself. Remind yourself regularly of the alternative means. Whatever decision you make, make it a commercial one.

Get started

Work with your team to isolate the aspects of your business that could benefit from an acquisition. Use the checklist in chapter 36 as a guide and build on it. Set parameters for the size of acquisition you think you could handle. Bear in mind the impact this will have on your bargaining position in future negotiations and the effect it could have on the equity you will have in the combined entity. Equity swaps are an attractive way of avoiding debt, but only at the expense of diluting the level of ownership held by existing owners. Understand the extent to which you may lose control *before* you make a deal.

Make this a scoping study. Build a range of alternative acquisitions. If you know of current opportunities or special situations (for example, where retiring founders may be interested in selling), include them on your list. Speak to business brokers about this review. You need not mention specific targets. The brokers will provide information; they will alert you to possibilities if they know you are open to new purchases.

Examine each possibility in terms of its fit with your own organisation, its culture, its profitability and its people. Develop criteria for judging suitability—including likely availability—and then rank your list of preferred targets.

You are still at a point where this is a confidential exercise shared with your immediate and trusted team only. Nonetheless, you can gather much intelligence from public sources. Delegate among yourselves the various tasks involved in gathering intelligence. Use the internet aggressively, analyse websites, review brochures and catalogues, and compare product pricing and market position. Later chapters in this book provide templates for competitive analysis and risk assessment. Use them at this stage to organise your thoughts.

Where appropriate, collect insights from customers and suppliers. What is the target doing that is better or worse than you can do? Both have potential. Can you lift their game, or yours, via acquisition? Are there clear synergies in marketing, production or the expense base?

How will it look?

Develop your own model of how the business would be integrated. What duplicated costs could be eliminated? What cross-selling could be generated from existing marketing outlays? What currently closed market segments could be opened to your current services?

You need to get a sense at this early stage of what the real benefits would be in financial terms. Start modelling this. It is only then that you can start to take a commercial view of just how much value would be added by the acquisition, and therefore what kind of investment is going to make sense. Remember that even if this turns into a merger in which no money changes hands, both businesses will have to be valued as a basis for working out the terms of that merger.

Examine the target in broad strategic terms as well. Where is it in the life cycle of a business? Is it at the 'bleeding edge' or the 'leading edge'? Are you acquiring it when its growth prospects are strong? It needn't be so. There are situations where the purchase of steady, recurrent earnings is exactly what a firm needs.

Finally, look closely at the tax aspects, not just in terms of the transaction, but also the implications for the combined entity. You must take professional advice here. The financial success of the strategy may well turn on this issue.

When you have reached a point where the proposed strategy has the advantage, check again that this is a sensible alternative to organic growth in terms of the three criteria: risk, cost and speed.

Talk to the potential target

If you have found that the target firm is open to offers or is already on the market, the way forward is clear. If not, as is often the case, your approach needs to be carefully considered. First impressions count, and the likelihood of proceeding to the next stage is often decided by how sensitively the initial stages are handled.

The chance of success in any business transaction is optimised when the proposition is a win for all parties. Set your team a brainstorming task: what's in it for the target?

Even if the target firm is a listed company, there must be a reason for shareholders to sell. That is generally price, but in hostile takeovers, there often needs to be more reason for boards to recommend acceptance. In the non-listed sector, this is even more acute. Equity is usually tightly held and there is little separation between ownership and management. The decision to sell or merge is usually in the hands of a few influential people, and they will not be swayed simply by price. In any case, the option of making a hostile bid in the unlisted sector is limited unless it solves fractious issues between owners—and while this might provide opportunities, their existence is not always a good sign.

So, what are the advantages to the target business?

To begin, look at your own reasons. By definition, synergies are mutually advantageous. The idea that you are both going to do well out of this is central to the scenario. In your first discussions, the focus should be on those positives. Are there areas where the other firm is struggling and where a joint strategy will lift its prospects? Do you have financial resources that could benefit the new company? Do you offer geographical advantages or access to market segments that provide new opportunities? Work through your own analysis viewing the proposition from the point of view of the other firm, its management and its shareholders.

Be conservatively realistic in your analysis. Overly optimistic scenarios will only question your credibility and generate a view of the combined entity that supports a price you may not be prepared to pay.

Be prepared for questions about how the combined entity will be managed. The moment the suggestion has been made, 'life after acquisition' will become central to the discussions. What opportunities are there for the existing owners, managers and employees? Be able to make it clear that you have considered this deeply and have looked at solutions to potential issues.

When you have prepared a case that is credible and honest, you are ready to talk. There are several ways you could go about it. It is best not to make a cold call yourself. An informal suggestion is best. If you know the key person well enough, find the opportunity to have this discussion. If not, work with a third party. It can be a business broker, your mentor, your lawyer, your accountant or other contacts (such as customers or suppliers who have a relationship with the person in question, or appropriate mutual acquaintances).

If none of these suit and you decide on a formal written approach, ensure that it is delivered directly to the person concerned. This is a confidential matter with ramifications for everyone involved in either firm. You do not want to lose the initiative through leaked information before you have even had a chance to outline the logic behind your proposal. You need not provide details of your strategy, but you need to make it clear that you think there are great opportunities for all concerned if the two firms were to work together. Then go on to suggest you meet and discuss the idea.

Due diligence

Failure to fully investigate an acquisition is a major cause of business collapse. For that reason, the notion of 'due diligence' is fully accepted as an essential part of the process. In addition, both directors and managers often have a legal responsibility to ensure the process is honest and thorough.

Once the two parties have agreed to proceed, they usually sign a confidentiality agreement, after which formal due diligence can begin. Your own team can now look closely at the business model, management, operations and marketing. Interviews with managers and key staff can take place. Your scoping study will have made it clear where you need to look and what you need to ask, be it to do with the quality of staff or assets, or the organisational structure and management of the firm.

For financial and legal aspects, however, you must use professionals. Have your accountant examine the books, not only to verify the performance, but also to search for potential savings and liabilities. Putting together a proforma set of accounts for the combined entity will highlight the opportunities for generating greater value.

Lawyers, whether you like them or not, are essential. You need to know the history of any legal issues the firm has faced or is facing. The terms of licensing agreements, patents or warranties need to be fully understood, as do any pending regulatory issues. You will also likely want to frame the final sale and purchase agreements such that you are effectively shielded from potential or unknown liabilities.

Is it worth it?

The business landscape is littered with firms that have failed by trying to grow by acquisition. Many mergers have been between firms for which there is simply no cultural fit, even in seemingly similar spaces. The horrendous track record of merging commercial banks with investment banks is largely due to massive cultural differences and totally opposing approaches to risk, one industry being based on avoiding risk and the other on taking it. The blurring of these lines is partly what brought Citibank to its knees in the sub-prime crisis.

Alternatively, the strategy has worked spectacularly well in situations where the fit has been fully explored, the acquisition has been carefully examined and the structure of the combined entity has been a win–win.

Whatever route you choose, just investigating the opportunity can be a rewarding way to work *on* your business as opposed to *in* it.

Examine the scenarios

If in this chapter you have identified a way in which your business could benefit from the purchase of another business, choose a potential target and examine the possibilities. Even if you prefer not to commit to a strategy of growth by acquisition, this exercise will help you see your business from a different and potentially innovative perspective. You will generate other interesting scenarios along the way, such as:

⋙ merging rather than acquiring
⋙ being acquired rather than acquiring
⋙ initiating marketing alliances with other firms
⋙ outsourcing part of your operations, and vice versa
⋙ joint venture opportunities
⋙ geographic diversification
⋙ ways of developing (or imitating) your competitors' strengths and addressing their weaknesses
⋙ ideas for working on your own.

38

Deal with crises

Acknowledge, assess, plan, communicate and act

Crises come out of nowhere. Like in a perfect storm, everything happens at once. Crises can be sparked by natural causes, human behaviour, or dramatic changes in the political or economic environment. Some can be anticipated. But when they occur, usually no-one has anticipated their intensity. Some give early warning signals, but no-one was watching—or if they were, they didn't act in time, or didn't act at all. Serious crises risk people's safety, damage property and equipment, and impact heavily on operations. Can we prepare for them? And what should we do when they happen?

With natural disasters, we have some experience. They happen regularly—so much so that we often have a standard response. The fire drill is a simple example. Our farm carries out a procedure at the beginning of the bushfire season. Fire pumps and hoses are checked and cleaned. Use and handling is practised by staff. There is a muster point where employees gather in case of emergency and from which any response is coordinated. Contingency plans are set up to cope with failure of power or water pressure. Staff are briefed on how to ensure their own safety.

In a bushfire-prone country this is standard procedure, yet many disastrous fires happen every year with great loss of life and property. This can reflect a lack of preparation, but more often than not, it is a result of a dramatic change in conditions, which brings about a level of intensity that wasn't expected. This is a fair definition of a crisis.

Crises in business

Where natural causes are the issue, there is often support from public emergency services, and (as with bushfires) there are well-known procedures for handling them. The sorts of crises we experience in business, however—and the ones we are addressing here—are often complicated events that impact on staff, operations, customers and finance. You rarely have the support of public services. You have to work with your own resources.

Some of the most common crises—such as cash flow problems, losing your biggest customer, a system crash with no backup or a walkout by key employees—are avoidable. Too often, early corrective action has simply not been taken. Even where attention has been paid to planning, the plans have just not been achievable, or the timelines imposed have been unrealistic. Other crises may arise from external causes beyond your control, such as major technological shifts, new competition, a collapse in trading conditions, and of course malicious behaviour by employees, competitors or enemies.

If you are facing any of these, clearly you want to avoid a panicked, unplanned response. The preferred approach might have been to brainstorm some critical scenarios ahead of time and develop a process to guide your response, just as you would with a fire drill. The best crisis management, after all, is managing to avoid crises. But glib clichés like that are easy to say when the crisis has already hit.

If it is too late for avoidance, you need to follow the steps outlined in any contingency plan. Normal operating procedures should be suspended and replaced with an emergency plan. You will need to act decisively and manage the response to the best of your ability. Each situation will be different, but there are some guidelines that can help.

Survive your crisis

First, another cliché, but an important one: do not panic. Morale will not improve if there are signs that you are not managing the situation. If your best sales team has just walked out, accept it, assess the situation and announce that you will be managing it.

Once when I was flying from London to Glasgow, our aircraft lost part of its undercarriage on lift-off from Heathrow. Noise from the incident made it clear to all of us on board that something was not right. The pilot's first announcement came shortly after. He acknowledged the incident and told us we would circle the airport while ground crews inspected the debris on the tarmac to ascertain the damage. He said he would speak to us again as soon as he fully understood the situation.

This short message did three things:

1   It acknowledged the situation.
2   It let us know that the pilot was taking steps to fully assess the implications.
3   It communicated the pilot's undertaking to keep us informed as soon as new information was available.

We circled for 20 minutes, flying low over Heathrow while controllers visually examined the plane with binoculars. Various other diagnostics were undertaken. We then levelled out and headed north.

The pilot came on air shortly after. He said that there definitely was damage to the starboard undercarriage. Various system checks had shown the plane to be functioning perfectly well in all other respects and that we would proceed to Glasgow. He said the plane was able to land with most weight on its nose wheel and port undercarriage and that he was trained to safely handle this sort of landing. Emergency ground crews had been assembled and were awaiting our arrival. In the meantime, cabin crew would again take us through the procedures for emergency evacuation, something we had all pretty much ignored when announced prior to the wheels falling off. This time, we paid attention.

Again, three things. This time:

1   The situation was explained.
2   The implications were outlined.
3   The crisis management plan was explained and we were told what our role would be.

In short, he was managing the crisis. Clearly, as I am here to tell the tale, we landed without incident. The passengers were not exactly calm throughout the flight, but we knew what to do and took comfort in the knowledge that there was a plan to manage the crisis. We were probably assisted by the decision to roll out the drinks trolley on a complimentary basis.

I have often remembered this event and the way it was handled. The process is reflected in the following guidelines:

1   *Acknowledge.* Affirm that there is a serious problem. It is probably clear to everyone, so there is no point in playing it down. People need to know that you are taking this very seriously and taking steps to address the situation. Communicate this clearly and positively to your staff.
2   *Assess.* While you may not have all the facts at this early stage, separate fear from reality and fact from fiction. Make an objective assessment on the basis of the information available. State clearly, on a step-by-step basis, what has gone wrong. When you put your management plan together, these steps will suggest the various actions you can take.
3   *Stay current.* Things change quickly. Ensure that any new information is immediately reported to you. This is essential. If, for example, a client is already reacting to a team departure, you need to know immediately. If your bank is reviewing your credit lines, focus on it now. Don't hope that it will pass.

4 *Collaborate.* Examine the implications. You can use help here. Our earlier suggestion of setting up a think tank to leverage recovery works just as well in critical times. Surround yourself with the people you need to manage this incident.

5 *Brainstorm scenarios.* Assess your position. Work with others to brainstorm the implications of the crisis. Acknowledge scenarios in which things could get worse and develop contingency plans for such events. Despite the setback, review the resources you have at your disposal and your areas of strength. Collectively examine your options for:

- containing the damage
- taking initiatives that will improve the situation
- implementing a recovery plan.

6 *Delegate.* When you have done this, communicate the response to everyone involved. Delegate responsibilities to the relevant people. Make it clear what you plan to do and what their roles are. If a complicated plan is required, break it down into simple steps. Explain the sequence and begin work on the first step.

7 *Communicate.* Throughout the crisis, keep open lines of communication with your key advisers and the staff in general. Provide regular updates of developments and, in particular, of progress. Crises breed uncertainty. The best antidote is for people to feel certain that the crisis is being managed.

When it has passed

You may have to deal with much of this process without much of a break, but when you have emerged from the crisis, review the entire incident. Carry out a crisis audit. You and your team are fresh from handling the issue. You are in a position to assess the effectiveness of the process and look at what could be done differently. Ask them to invent different critical scenarios and then work through the process to see what developments might be preventable and how others could be better managed.

If you are lucky enough not to have had to deal with a critical situation, spend an hour thinking of one now. You might be surprised not only at where you are vulnerable to a crisis, but also at the resources you have — or don't have — to handle it.

Analyse your competition
Identify your competitive edge

No business has a monopoly on the best ideas. Many things you are doing are best practice, but there will always be areas where someone else is performing better. It can be for any number of reasons: simple things like location, time in the market, technological advantages, better management, targeted customer service and stronger training; or it could be due to something special and exclusive to them, or you.

To focus on your competitors is not to ignore your strengths. Rather, it will clarify whether your particular practices really are strengths relative to the competition. If they are, it will lead you to strategies to help drive home the competitive edge that those strengths give you. If they are not, it will open doors to practices that you are either not doing now, or not doing well, and prompt actions to address them.

Stay at the leading edge

This is a great exercise for any people who are serious about the profitability, survival and growth of their businesses. It is a perfect task for your think tank. It should not be a one-off project. It is a dynamic process that requires regular review in rapidly changing environments. The one thing you can be sure of is that once you develop a fantastically competitive innovation, it will be immediately copied by someone else.

The opposite is obviously also true. If you are constantly monitoring your competitors and are aware of their capabilities, you are less likely to be blindsided by an initiative on their part. You will be in a position to respond quickly to new challenges.

Start this process by working out just who your competitors are. This might not be as obvious as it sounds. You may sell cakes through a well-positioned outlet in a shopping mall. But so does another operator eight shops down the row. Okay, so they are a direct competitor. But the supermarket that drives the traffic past your store also sells cakes. And so does a bakery that isn't even in the mall. And for that matter, the chocolate shop opposite seems to have a lot of customers in common with you. Competitive analysis is not just about who is in direct competition with you. It is about who is getting the biggest 'share of the wallet' that is available to you.

Your customer base determines your competitive position. You might sell books to people who love browsing in bookshops. But others just buy on Amazon. What can you do about that? By looking beyond your direct competitors, you can generate a far wider range of ideas to sharpen your competitive edge. So when you put together your list of who you will analyse, don't just include the most direct examples. Cast around for those indirect competitors who attract business from customers that might otherwise have come to you.

Don't be put off by a lack of information. Any enterprising team can quickly think of ways of performing due diligence on your competitors. These could include any of the following actions:

> Thoroughly check competitors' websites.
> Examine their brochures and handouts.
> Analyse their advertising and marketing policies.
> Carefully scrutinise their actual ads and promotions.
> Have frank discussions with your customers and theirs.
> Use mystery shoppers or enquirers to rate the customer experience of your business and the competitors'.
> Use customer surveys to determine what you are not providing in your own business.
> Maintain communication channels with your suppliers. Know what they are doing for the opposition.

▷ Go to industry trade shows and seminars.
▷ Monitor newspaper articles, analysts' reports and trade magazines.
▷ Check the competitors' annual accounts and regulatory filings.
▷ Have your sales team investigate further.

How do you want to compare?

Once you have your target list, identify the criteria you want to use in the comparison. Twelve areas are suggested in the following paragraphs and are listed in table 39.1, which you could use as a template. Give your firm and the other firms percentage ratings and list the relevant strengths and weaknesses. You can make this a big project, investigating further over time; however, just making an intuitive check now will sharpen your perspective on your market position.

Table 39.1: a competitor comparison template

Key factors	You (%)	Strengths/ weaknesses	Firm A	Strengths/ weaknesses	Firm B	Strengths/ weaknesses
Product						
Pricing						
Customer service						
Reputation and image						
Presentation						
Sales and marketing						
Terms and conditions						

Table 39.1 *(cont'd)*: a competitor comparison template

Key factors	You (%)	Strengths/ weaknesses	Firm A	Strengths/ weaknesses	Firm B	Strengths/ weaknesses
Growth strategy						
Flexibility						
Technology						
Financial strength						
Future strategy						

Product

What are the strengths and weaknesses of your product? Is quality a key characteristic? Does it need to be? Would a simplified model generate greater sales with a better profit margin? How do you rate the competition's product or service? Do you need to copy some aspects of theirs or, alternatively, improve the way in which yours differentiates itself in the marketplace? Minor changes in product design can often have a disproportionate influence on market appeal. Is the design consistent? Does it meet users' expectations? Is labelling clear? Is your website easily navigated in a way that others are?

Pricing

Is your pricing policy scientific? Businesses often have a standard markup equation. Have you examined yours lately? What is the actual profitability of different product lines? Think 80:20. Does penetration of a particular market segment require more aggressive pricing, which would not only boost sales numbers but would do so in your strongest suit? Do your competitors have different pricing structures? Are some overpriced in a way that offers you an opportunity, or do they consistently beat you on price? Why is that? What are they doing that gives them a price advantage? Can you collaborate with particular distributors, or suppliers, in order to price more aggressively?

Customer service

Ask around. You don't often hear about how good a particular company's customer service is, but you will definitely hear about it if it is poor. How long will it be before firms understand that being left on permanent hold on a voice-activated 1300 number — only to be transferred to wait in another queue — has an exponentially negative impact on their customer rankings? It doesn't matter how good the management team is; if the experience is bad at the coalface, it's bad for the entire firm.

Because the negatives are well broadcast, it can take a bit of investigation to find out where customers are keen to shop. Try being the mystery shopper or client yourself. It is not simply a retail issue. Your preferred lawyer is invariably the one who gets back to you promptly. The best stockbroker I knew was not brilliant at investment analysis, but she made sure that any query from a client — even the hint of one — was answered almost instantly. It meant harassing her colleagues for answers, but it also meant maintaining a long list of loyal clients. As one said to me, 'If I want something done, I get her to do it because I know it will be done in a flash. I'm happy to pay for that.' Our share of that client's wallet consistently exceeded our competitor's share by a wide margin.

Success in this area comes from incorporating customer service into your business culture. In a later chapter, you will develop a 'unique selling proposition' (USP). This is a clear statement of what makes you special. What's yours? Are your competitors clearer or more focused on this? People buy goods and services to find a solution — something that solves their problem or makes them feel good. What problem or need can your solution address? Exactly what problem do you solve?

Who solves it better? Customer service ultimately appeals to the client at an emotional level. How do you rate the customer experience when dealing with your firm and with a competitor? For example, is it fast, thorough, punctual, well presented, reliable, friendly, experienced or businesslike? I go back to a particular chemist in my area not because it is the cheapest but because it is just a pleasure to walk in there. If I can't get through to my accountant on the first call, I know he will call back as soon as he is free. Always. Why would I change?

Reputation and image

What do you think of when the name of a competitor is mentioned? What words come to mind? Are they images that are stronger or weaker than for your firm? Why is that so? Reputation and image are generated and maintained by consistency. Do you have policies in place to help maintain your market position over time by ensuring that your firm is always presented in the manner you want it to be perceived? This can include anything from staff presentation and helpfulness through to friendliness, cleanliness and reliability.

Presentation

Does your presentation align with your market position? I buy secondhand utes for my horse business. I don't expect a luxury customer lounge at the car yard. I want proof of reliability, service history and functionality of the vehicle. That's what I received when I bought my last one, and so that is where I'll go back. My personal car, on the other hand, is a quality foreign make. When I go to either purchase or service the vehicle, I expect, and receive, very polished attention. If I have to wait to pick it up after a service, it will be on a comfortable sofa, reading a newspaper while I sip my free cappuccino. If the service experience was reversed, my expectations would not be met. Luxury service at the used car yard would make me suspicious. Lean and grubby service at the luxury showroom would make me think these people are not up to the required standard. Do your competitors have this right? Do you?

Sales and marketing

Name a competitor and think of their advertising or promotional campaigns. What's the first one that comes to mind? By definition, that will be what they are doing right. What is it about that item that made it stick in your mind? How do you rate it against your own efforts? What can you do about it? Do they have sales practices that extend their coverage? Do they run excellent telemarketing campaigns? Are they on top of online promotion and selling? Is their website so optimised that it always appears ahead of yours? Is their sales team better trained? Have they launched unique campaigns? Are they better staffed? Are you relatively understaffed?

Terms and conditions

Do your competitors have stronger ties with suppliers, or terms and conditions that give them better margins or pricing power? Equally, do they offer their customers more flexible payment terms or delivery options? Your own credit policy, if you have one, can be a vehicle for attracting and maintaining your customer base.

Growth strategy

Which competitor seems to be growing more quickly? Not just in terms of sales, but in terms of product range and new ideas? Is someone leveraging their business into new and profitable market segments? Are they doing it organically and building on their existing operations, or are they doing it by collaborating with others? Are competitors forming alliances, merging with others, buying sales teams or taking over rivals? What is your growth policy at the strategic level?

Flexibility

How quickly do others respond to changed conditions? Are they more flexible than your firm when the economic or market environment shifts? Are they quicker to introduce new lines? Is speed to market a strength or a weakness? Is your focus on what you are currently doing, or do you take time to work with your team on new ideas and strategies? The failure of most great businesses is a failure to adapt.

Technology

This area changes very quickly for any business. Whether it is the quality of your customer relations management system, your inventory monitoring, your production processes, your financial software or any other aspect of business, this is where the speed of innovation is almost overwhelming. And it is an area in which to be wary. The most common complaint about fantastic IT solutions is that they fail to deliver the promised result. IT by its nature is based on mathematics and logic, so the plan and the solution always appear to be extremely rational. Not so, however, is the implementation, training and synchronicity with your business practices. What should you do? Being an early adopter can shift you to the front of the pack, but it can also cost you dearly. Carefully examine what is working for your competitors, but make sure you keep a close eye on what didn't work and why.

Financial strength

How's yours? Do key competitors enjoy stronger financial backing? How could you rectify that? Do you need partners? Do they have them? How is their funding structured? Do they use leasing or other means to give them greater flexibility? What options do you have?

Future strategy

Who is best placed to take advantage of future developments? Would the introduction of new products threaten your revenue base? Do others seem to be continually ahead of the game? Why is that so? How does your culture compare in this area? Do your ongoing business practices include allocations of both time and resources to planning the future development of your products and services?

Complete and use your comparison

A review like this can turn into a major project. Start with areas that need attention. You may want to make your own analytical table or put it up on a whiteboard as you work with your team. But make sure you include the strengths and weaknesses of your own business in the process. When you look at others, don't lose sight of what you are already doing well.

When you rank a competitor higher or lower than your firm, note their relevant strengths or weaknesses. When you have done the analysis, identify areas where you can gain advantage by emulating the strength of another, or, equally, where your own strength may assist you to exploit the weakness of another.

Your investigation may reveal many ideas and opportunities, but as we have stressed throughout this book, identify at least one that is simple, doable and can generate a result. That's the one to start now.

Monitor your performance targets

Integrate KPIs into your business

How often does this happen? You have a great team meeting or an uplifting seminar. The ideas are good. Everyone knows what needs to change. People are reinvigorated. There's lots of talk about moving forward and a general sense that things are going to be different.

All good stuff. A week later some new behaviours have emerged; even some new products and strategies seem to be implemented. The next week, though, the momentum starts to flag. By the end of the month, the mood is back to normal. Six months later, management is talking about the need for motivation. There's a call for an inspirational strategy session to really get things moving.

What happened?

Nothing changes if nothing changes

Two things hold back the implementation of inspirational change. One is the tendency to end an uplifting weekend with revised aims and objectives, new value frameworks and fresh mission statements. Everything except real action. The bar has been raised so high with ideas that they overwhelm the small steps you need to take get things moving.

The second is the failure to implement a follow-up system to ensure things actually change. Regardless of the type of change you want to institute, it needs to be specified in terms of targets, timelines and measures. That's what should come from your planning session. It doesn't have to be complicated. Small steps are required. The fewer there are, the more likely it is that something will happen. Then to keep it happening, you need to monitor the progress. Welcome to KPIs.

Key performance indicators

'Key performance indicators' (KPIs) are very simple: they mean what they say. They are indicators of how you are performing in areas that are key to fulfilling your mission.

A more evolved version of KPIs is the 'balanced scorecard', in which the indicators are derived from, and integrated into, the overall goals of your firm. They work best when they monitor not only performance, but also strategies to improve performance. Other similar tools — such as 'strategy maps' and 'critical success factors' (CSFs) — aim for the same result. We will use the term KPI to refer to all forms of monitoring in this section.

A simple KPI already exists in many firms: the sales target. Each salesperson has a monthly goal in financial terms. This is compared with his or her actual performance, and the variance between the two indicates how sales are going relative to the budget. A more elaborate KPI has two advantages:

1   It can help investigate why performance is ahead or behind.
2   It monitors efforts to improve performance, relating those efforts to the overall management of the business.

In other words, it is not simply a financial indicator. It is a core part of the firm's implementation strategy.

Set up effective monitoring

To introduce a comprehensive monitoring framework, you need to answer three basic questions:

1   Where do you want to go?
2   What goals do you have to achieve to get there?
3   What do you need to do to achieve those goals?

Work through a simple example. Alpha Business Services (ABS) is a medium-sized advisory firm. It has its roots in accounting services, but has grown to offer its client base a broad range of financial products including leasing, mortgage broking, personal loans and superannuation advice.

ABS has developed a clear mission for the business: become the premier advisory firm in its target market. To achieve that mission, the company held a weekend strategy session at a fashionable resort. Yes, there was a round of golf, but by Saturday night they had identified the following goals:

⇨ Offer a full range of services to existing clients.
⇨ Boost market share by expanding the client base and product range.
⇨ Maintain a high level of customer satisfaction.
⇨ Lift the level of repeat and referral business.
⇨ Double net revenues over a five-year period.

On Sunday morning, they began translating this overall vision into operational goals. They wanted to quantify their achievement and link it to individual performance. They did this by breaking down each one in line with the perspectives typically used in balanced scorecards: financial, customers, internal processes, and innovation and learning. These guidelines can be applied to any business.

Financial

Start with a snapshot of the firm's current performance. What is the turnover in each product category? What is the expense base and what is the margin? What is the current return on investment? What is the number of customers required in each category to achieve your current budget? Having established this, what is the growth rate required over time to lift revenue to the target level? Working back from this, what are the KPIs for each sales unit in each product that collectively move you towards your goal?

The financial perspective can cover a wide variety of goals. It may be an EBITDA or cash flow target, a maintenance target based around sustainability, a growth target or even a strategy for survival.

Customers

How satisfied are customers? What is the complaint rate? Do you survey their ratings of your service? Do you have a high level of unique clients? What about the level of referral business, lead generation, lead conversion and repeat business? These are decisive indicators for fine-tuning performance.

What changes can you make and how can you monitor them?

Internal processes

Can the delivery system be improved? Do you have the best suppliers? Are the right assets allocated to the right areas? Does poor inventory management tie up funds and increase your cost of capital? Can you improve your payment terms or shrink the extent of ageing receivables? Are reporting lines clear, simple and functional?

Innovation and learning

What are the additional skills or systems required to reach your goals? Do the sales team need more training? Does your customer relations management system meet your requirements? What new products, or product derivatives, can you add to your range?

Would broader learning shift the firm's culture in a new direction? If so, what is to be implemented, by whom and by when?

Follow it through

Let's return to our example. ABS has developed KPIs across its operations but has realised it needs more product. One opportunity it identified was reverse mortgages. These are simply credit lines against property that can be drawn down over time. Instead of paying down debt, the owner increases debt and services the interest. ABS clients looked to the service to offset short-term falls in superannuation income arising from the GFC.

ABS examined the investment in terms of the financial targets it had to meet and the number and type of customers it had to attract to reach those goals. There was also the implementation of any new internal process that was needed to back up the product, along with marketing and the training and innovations that would support the project. The result was the monthly monitoring report shown in table 40.1 (on pages 224 to 225).

The report might appear complicated, but it brings together the critical indicators to monitor the success of this new venture. By reviewing it line by line, you can see a call to action in each item.

For example, the estimated number of leads generated internally from existing business relationships and data was about right, but new lead generation was 12.9 per cent below expectations. Greater emphasis on buying databases may address this.

The conversion rate is low, but sales training in this area is planned. Referrals are good, suggesting service levels are being maintained. Repeat clients was likely an overestimate, given the nature of the product. Stronger unsolicited clients suggests promotional activity is working. Margins are up with more focus on larger clients. This month, revenue is ahead of budget.

In the customer perspective, the advertising spend is below budget, but these funds can be diverted to database purchases.

Planning for the quarterly promotional seminar is underway. The immediate postcode has been covered with a mail drop and each month the relevant page on the website has been updated. It is suggested that email marketing be doubled using funds from the advertising budget with the aim of lifting the number of new leads.

On the internal processes, progress is slow, but it is being monitored and action is being taken. In terms of innovation and learning, there is progress, but the sales training that might lift the conversion rate has not happened. It is now scheduled for the coming month. The point is, it has been highlighted, acted upon and scheduled to actually take place.

Use KPIs

KPIs can be introduced across any business. While they can focus on individual or product performance, they can also be used in scorecards that show the overall performance of the firm. This is an extremely useful management tool. On one hand, they can be aggregated to show the whole picture; on the other, they enable management to quickly identify what is behind the performance, or for that matter, what is not. Creating them is not difficult. The example here was put together on a spreadsheet. Excellent off-the-shelf software can be downloaded from the web. If you type KPI into any search engine, you will find no shortage of material, much of it free. Using a KPI process will do two things:

1   It will allow you to focus on the actual outcomes that strategy sessions are meant to lead to, not just the broad aims and objectives.
2   It will set up a system that not only triggers action, but also maintains the momentum behind all those great ideas.

Table 40.1: monthly monitoring report

Indicator	Last month actual	This month target	This month actual	Variance	Comments
Financial					
Internal leads	152	150	143	−4.7%	Okay
New leads	380	450	392	−12.9%	Spend more on databases
Total leads	532	600	535	−10.8%	
Conversion rate	0.75%	0.65%	0.56%	−14%	Conversion training ongoing
Leads converted	4	3.9	3	−23%	
Referrals	1	0.25	1	300%	Better than expected
Repeat clients	0	1	0	−100%	Overestimated?
Unsolicited customers	1	0.5	2	300%	Promotions working
Number of sales	6	5.65	6	6.2%	
Average margin ($)	2890	3750	3985	6.3%	Focus on bigger clients
Monthly income ($)	17 340	21 188	23 910	12.8%	Okay

Indicator	Last month actual	This month target	This month actual	Variance	Comments
Customer					
Advertising ($)	500	1000	750	−25.0%	Underspent; divert to database
Seminar		Quarterly			Planning underway; venue booked
Monthly promotion		Mailbox			Immediate postcode covered; monitoring
Website marketing		Update			Done
Email marketing	500	500	500		Use ad budget to double data purchase
Internal processes	Rating		Action		
Adaptation of CRM	60%	System installed; 40% of data still to be uploaded			
New accounting	45%	Integration problems with existing system			
Add new supplier	0%	No progress; discussions with new supplier scheduled next month			
Innovation and learning					
Train support staff	85%	Okay, but needs more practice			
Sales training	0%	Scheduling problems; time set aside next month			

41

Manage your risk
Review what could go wrong

It is too late to insure your premises when the building is on fire. Catastrophic events are rarely preventable and hardly predictable. You can prepare for them beforehand and you can manage them when they happen. But as for predicting them, the best you can do is take a chance on probability.

Risk management has been the fashion in the wake of the GFC. Because the crisis came with such force and such speed, it highlighted the frailties of systems that had been put in place to counter such an event. The irony was that many of the derivative products hailed as insurance against risk proved to be the undoing of the financial system rather than its saviour. Hedging strategies make rational mathematical sense, but if the market seizes up and you can't implement them, they have a multiplier effect on the crisis they were meant to help you avoid.

The GFC was a perfect storm. Whatever could go wrong did—all at once. There was nowhere to hide. Crises can occur in any business, and it is rare that they stop with one triggering incident. Usually that initial event will bring about issues elsewhere in the business at a time when resources are already stretched. You might lose a key sales team just when the opposition is mounting a competitive new product. Economic conditions could deteriorate at the same time as the bank is reviewing your overdraft terms. The recession could drive your key supplier out of business and your strongest customer might move to a rival to ensure reliable delivery.

Look for likely dominoes

An unravelling like this makes it clear that you cannot assess your risk by looking at different functions in isolation. A firm has an ecology that ensures an impact in one area will ultimately affect operations in another. You need to examine your risk exposure on a holistic, firm-wide basis.

To do this, look at whole scenarios, not just individual events. Review your exposure from four perspectives:

1 trigger events
2 probability
3 consequences
4 reducing risk.

What sets off a crisis?

Triggers can be within your control or outside it. Natural disasters like fire and flood are outside your control but can be mitigated by insurance and preventive measures. By definition, you have little warning of their arrival. Triggers within your control can more easily be anticipated by a careful review of the nature of your business. The same notions of insurance and prevention can be applied to your preparation for them.

Examine your business risk in the following areas, but take care to see where a problem in one area could cascade into another. Such risks may not be eliminated, but you can take steps to minimise them. Some strategies are suggested in each category.

Financial

How exposed are you to interest rates? Do existing debt levels give you room to move? Does demand for your product relate to conditions in financial or stock markets? Are revenues too dependent on a small number of customers? What would happen if those customers moved or went out of business?

Possible strategies

▷ Stress-test your leverage and manage it to a lower level if appropriate.

▷ Diversify your credit lines.

▷ Aggressively seek new customers.

▷ Look for business lines that are counter-cyclical.

Market

Look at competitive conditions. Imagine the arrival of new and better products, well-funded new entrants, changing consumer preferences or shifts in payment and ordering processes.

Possible strategies

▷ Further differentiate your product lines.

▷ Tie in key customers with preferred terms and conditions.

▷ Introduce loyalty programs.

▷ Examine suitability of new technology.

Operational

Consider failure of production processes, failure of new product, loss of key personnel, health and safety issues, and a radical change in the technology behind your manufacturing processes or service provision.

Possible strategies

▷ Make quality management a specific objective.

▷ Put someone in charge of quality management and establish a quarterly review.

▷ Examine the entire risk profile of new initiatives and products.

Regulatory

Compliance can be a thorny issue, especially for small businesses. Nonetheless, workplace and product regulations are a reality. Most agencies provide guidelines to check the status of your operations. Also include here your exposure to legal risk—from the likelihood of being sued by a customer through to ensuring your firm is legally structured in a way that minimises the impact of adverse developments.

Possible strategies

⇨ Set up a checklist of all regulations affecting your business and schedule a timetable for reviewing the list.

⇨ Examine the use of different incorporations to establish firewalls that stop problems in one business segment flowing into another.

Natural

What is the likelihood of a natural disaster impacting on your business? Don't just think about the obvious fires and floods. What does an unseasonably wet period do to your business? What about a prolonged dry one?

Possible strategies

⇨ Obviously, insurance is one risk management tool in this area, but so is the extent and implementation of maintenance programs or exercise drills on what to do in case of emergencies. See chapter 38.

People

People are your most important assets. Are you overly dependent on any one person or team? Are you properly fireproofed against fraud, theft and reputation risk?

Possible strategies

☞ Ensure you have sound financial controls to minimise fraud.

☞ Look into incentive and status packages to boost the loyalty of key people.

☞ Hold training sessions that communicate the culture and mission of the firm to all employees.

☞ Look for buy-in on the benefits of boosting or maintaining the reputation of the firm.

How likely is it?

Don't lose sight of the probability of the event. This takes some careful analysis. In the case of insurable events, underwriters and actuaries draw on extensive histories of actual occurrences. The inverse of the insurance premium is usually a good indication of probability. For example, in my horse business, it costs between 2 per cent and 3 per cent to insure a broodmare. That is made up of an estimate of the probability of losing the broodmare plus an underwriter's markup.

It turns out to be close to the mark. On an annualised basis, I have lost about 2 out of 100 mares. The same logic applies to flood or fire cover. At the same time, be realistic. If your premises are on high ground in a dry area, flood is probably not an issue. But beware the burst water main or internal piping, or the vulnerability of customers and suppliers.

What is the impact?

The impact can often be expressed in monetary terms. Exactly how much custom do you think a top salesperson will take when leaving? What is the penalty you will pay for a compliance failure? What is the cost of a 1 per cent increase in the interest rate on your credit line? How much market share would you lose to a new entrant?

What about follow-on effects? What does the departure of a key employee do to morale? Will more follow? How does compliance or product failure affect your reputation? Work through the full scenario to assess the overall impact and the related issues you will have to address.

Make risk reduction a mindset

Other risks are less tangible. As a manager, you will probably be aware of the level of loyalty your firm commands, or the quality of your customer relations. Use your sense for these to rate your risk in each area. This is a productive exercise, because it will not only focus your risk management — it will highlight issues that you should be managing in any case.

It may not be possible to precisely forecast the probability of many external events, but you can often gauge the odds of an event happening. For example, legislative changes promised by an opposition party may impact on your business, but numerous polls will start forecasting their electoral prospects well in advance of a change of government.

Recessions happen every six to seven years. How long has it been since the last one? How did you handle it? What did you learn that can prepare you for the next one?

There may be nothing on the horizon, but there rarely is ahead of a perfect storm. The Australian stock market posted an annual gain in the four financial years leading up to June 2007. That hadn't happened in living memory. You don't have to be brilliant to have calculated that the odds on the upside were narrowing. Still, very few saw it coming, or if they did, few took action to offset the impact.

There is no faultless approach to reducing risk in your business. Some of the strategies listed earlier are obvious. Others will become clear to you once you develop your scenarios based on various triggers, then assess their probability and impact. It will help if you bear in mind several key principles of risk management:

1 *Dynamic monitoring.* The business environment can change quickly. Review your risk exposure regularly. Keep asking: 'What are the knock-on effects?'
2 *Communication.* Make all employees risk-aware. Ensure that potential problems are identified early. Have your think tank perform a risk review.
3 *Tolerance.* Stress-test your operations and your structure. How would they cope with changed conditions? Natural cushions such as spare capacity or unused financial resources are often squeezed in prosperity; equally, they can quickly evaporate in tough times.
4 *Recovery skills.* How quickly can you reverse the impact of the event? Do you have resources available to implement counter measures?
5 *Contingency plans.* Use scenario analysis to work up your response and examine the risk in the contingency plan itself.
6 *Liquidity.* This is generally a financial term indicating how quickly you can cut your losses, but it applies to any problem. How easily can you exit the situation? Does the exit door close in extreme conditions?
7 *Maintenance.* Apply this not only to physical assets. Check the maintenance of your relationships with staff, customers, suppliers, shareholders and the community in which you operate.

Assessing business risk is a process that applies to any business. Even one hour spent reviewing your business along these lines will quickly identify your firm's strengths and weaknesses. Think it through ahead of the fire.

Are you growing or ageing?

Where you are in the life cycle of your
business?

In 1960, there were six major department stores in Sydney: Marcus Clark, Mark Foys, Farmers, Anthony Horderns, Grace Bros and David Jones. Their business models were based on massive buildings in the CBD. By the 1970s, only two of the six were left. Some went into decline and disappeared entirely. Others merged or were taken over. Today, large-scale, department-store retailing is dominated by only two brands via a country-wide network of stores. The anchor tenants in any mall now are invariably David Jones and Myer. They in turn have lost market share to Harvey Norman and other discount retailers. Harvey Norman didn't exist in 1960. Nor, for that matter, did malls.

What happened? Was it one of the catastrophic events we referred to in chapter 41? No; it was just another dynamic that can both support and threaten the outlook for any business — the life cycle of the business itself.

Just as recessions come and go, so do products and so do firms. The cycles may vary in length or intensity, but they have identifiable phases with common characteristics. These phases — start-up, growth, maturity and decline — are shown in figure 42.1 (overleaf). Where you are in the cycle has ramifications for what your business strategy should be.

This is not a radical idea. Marketing strategists have long based their tactics on where a particular commodity is in the product life cycle. Business is no different.

233

Figure 42.1: the cycle of business

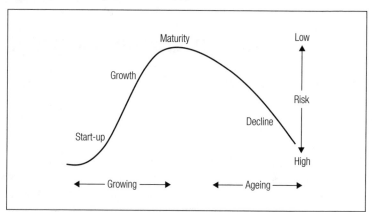

Where do you aim to be?

How many business plans have you seen that forecast a new venture to remain in 'early stage growth' for its entire life? On the contrary, most entrepreneurs want their businesses to evolve into stable enterprises that generate healthy, recurrent returns. That is an admirable goal, but its achievement brings with it a new set of challenges: how to ensure the growth and sustainability. Risk is high during the start-up stage, but the mature business also faces high risk during decline.

Start-up

Acknowledging the business life cycle is a little like acknowledging your own life. The start-up, or entrepreneurial stage, is not unlike adolescence: a time of high energy, a preparedness to take risks and that wonderful teenage quality of feeling bulletproof.

Of course, like a lot of teenagers, the business may run off the rails. But it is not for want of passion, risk-taking and confidence. The start-up period can be exciting; it is characterised by aggressive marketing, openness to new ideas, simplicity in product ranges and processes, and the availability of new markets with few competitors. At the same time, cash is usually king in these early days. Start-ups are regularly undercapitalised, and while running a business on the smell of an oily rag has its appeal, it is lack of cash that kills most new businesses launched in Australia. Generating cash flow is the prime objective in the early stage.

Growth

If the venture turns out to be a good idea and moves beyond the start-up stage, it won't be long before the competition intensifies. Like nature, the market detests a vacuum. There will soon be a competitor for your best idea. The growth stage is also a buoyant time of optimism and growing returns. But all the entrepreneurial skills required to launch the business now need to be applied to the management of the apparent success and the maintenance of the firm's competitive position.

It is often at this point that new entrepreneurs have their first wake-up call: suddenly they have to manage people and they are surprised, often even angry, to find that not everyone is motivated by the same goals as the business owner or creator.

The growth stage will not simply flourish on the rising tide of the successful start-up; it requires more focus and structure. Increased competition means that sales growth will slow and product or service differentiation strategies will be needed to maintain a competitive edge. Branding becomes a key focus as you try to lock in your market position. Nonetheless, steady sales volume provides more resources for product development and improving processes. Greater attention will be required in terms of staff and team management, and the sustainable business will establish a viable culture that supports employee motivation and loyalty.

Maturity

If the firm has managed its growth stage well, it invariably moves on to a mature platform. This is both good and bad. An established market position gives financial and industrial clout. These strengths can be marshalled to back new initiatives and opportunities so that the firm can diversify both vertically and horizontally. These advantages must be maintained, because now there are plenty of competitors vying for your space. Properly managed, the mature stage can evolve as a sustainable enterprise, but only if the firm continues to adapt.

The downside is, of course, that systems put in place to optimise productivity or profitability, or to minimise risk, can become embedded in business practices to the extent that they smother the enthusiasm and energy that has established those strengths in the first place. Complacency and inertia have seen many leading brands and businesses simply disappear over time.

Although sustainability becomes an objective in the mature stage, it is often at the cost of vision. Vision cannot be static. It needs to adapt to changing conditions. Look at the evolution of supermarkets.

The Woolworths stores of my youth sold no food. These large shops were located on suburban main streets. They were 'variety' stores in which a massive range of household and personal products were sold at competitive prices. Today, those product lines are confined to maybe one or two aisles in brightly lit, 30-aisle supermarkets, usually in malls that provide one-stop shopping with easy parking. Woolworths continue to use their position to encroach on other markets. These include banking via cash-out services and loyalty cards that encourage customers to purchase from their growing networks of petrol stations, which in turn sell products that are competitively sourced on the back of their supermarket buying clout. How's that for adaptation?

Decline

The mature stage may last a very long time, but there is no shortage of firms that do not adapt to changing conditions and eventually fall into the last stage: decline. By now, customer preferences have moved against them, and fashion has shifted dramatically. Technological change might have undermined their competitive edge; sales are falling and their products and services are generally provided more attractively through a range of rivals. In their core business, their strategic choices are limited. A fundamental shift in their business model is required, but that is now far more risky. Management inertia and entrenched thinking works against the dramatic change that is required.

The potential for rebirth

Such firms are often not without assets or opportunities. Cash flow may be under pressure, but the firms may have unprofitable yet highly valuable real estate holdings. Many have underused distribution channels and retail networks that could be applied to different activities. This is the reason 'change management' has become such a key part of the management skill set. Shifts in the business environment are now so rapid that a process of continual evolution is a strategy in itself.

Change management often requires a firm to return to the practices that characterised its operations in the start-up or growth stage. It is about breaking the mould and coming up with a completely new business model rather than putting a few bandaids around the existing one. This in itself is a start-up notion. Some much-loved product lines need to be eliminated entirely. Resources must be moved to projects that address new market development. Such strategies have more of the features of a start-up firm than a mature one.

Strategies for the life cycle

The life cycle of a business, then, suggests that different strategies are needed for different points in the cycle. Where are you, and what should you do? What are the characteristics of your operation, and what are the strategies that fit with your current profile?

Table 42.1 includes some areas you can examine. You will think of others. Look at your firm's history, its present position and its future. What actions should you be taking to ensure growth and sustainability? What worked in the past, and what needs to happen in the future?

Table 42.1: characteristics of and strategies for the phases of the business cycle

Stage	Characteristics	Actions and strategy
1 Start-up	Capital and cash flow are limited Markets are relatively open Risk is high Product range is narrow and uncomplicated	Target turnover, not profit Focus heavily on sales growth Try novel marketing initiatives Build distribution channels/outlets
2 Growth	New competitors arrive Cash flow is stronger Rate of sales growth eases Management issues arise	Focus on branding Expand/diversify product range Differentiate products and services Ensure internal processes are properly staffed
3 Maturity	Market is saturated Product range is broad Market position is strong Internal processes are established	Make constant promotion a priority Acquire new business lines Buy distribution or supply channels Review management; test new ideas

Stage	Characteristics	Actions and strategy
4 Decline	Sales are falling	Cut costs and harvest volume
	Customers are finding substitute products	Liquidate unprofitable assets
	Internal processes hinder change	Merge; be acquired; reinvent
	Firm is slow to adapt to market shifts	Eliminate 80; focus on 20

43

Use limited resources

Make things happen on a tight budget

Most business failures are due to a lack of cash. Yet so many businesses, especially start-ups, acknowledge the issue but do little to address it in practice. They talk the talk, but don't walk the walk. It is an easy trap to fall into. You have an idea. You are excited. You start working on it and before you know it, you are short of cash and your seed capital is exhausted.

There are three things to do about this. They are all 'musts':

1 You *must* set up a budget and monitor it against reality constantly.
2 You *must* aim to generate income, no matter how little, as soon as possible.
3 You *must* try to do as much as you can for as little as you can.

Budget for cash and profit

Constructing a budget for either a new business or a new project is standard practice. Spreadsheet technology has made this a fairly easy task, especially for running 'what if' scenarios. You may remember we discussed this in chapter 23, and a working template can be downloaded from <www.alanhargreaves.com>. Just remember one thing about spreadsheets: they are very easy to tweak. That makes it easy to test how your bottom line might look, but it also makes it easy to get the bottom line you like the look of. Avoid the temptation to fudge it.

A budget is only as useful as the information injected into it. The numbers have to be realistic. There is a tendency to focus budget thinking on expenses, whereas income is at least as important. Start with your revenue projections. The business is only going to work if it generates income. Realistically, how many more customers or sales is your new promotion going to bring in? Exactly how many units of your new product or service will you be able to sell, at what price, and, crucially, when? Plan for bad debtors, late payers and unforeseen contingencies. Three basic 'rules' of any new project are:

1   It will take longer than expected.
2   It won't go to plan.
3   It will cost more than first calculated.

Once you are happy with your revenue targets, look at what it will cost to reach them. One way is to add up the cost and raise the funds. That's good if you have the money, or you can find it.

Alternatively, you can take a more disciplined approach and decide what amount of capital you are prepared to make available. If you are unsure you want to commit that much — or simply can't guarantee you will have it — use the notion of affordable loss. What is the amount you are prepared to risk?

Using this number, what can you afford to do? This limited-budget approach injects serious financial discipline into your thinking. Start by listing the resources you require and then go through them one by one, examining each in terms of how cheaply you can put them in place.

Use your time

The first resource may be your time. How much of it can you commit? Maybe you have a lot available, or maybe it is limited to your evenings, or a certain number of your working hours. What does it add up to? Realistically, what can you achieve with the number of hours you have available? Make a timeline of your input and see where it leads you in terms of milestones on the way to reaching your target.

This can be sobering. When I first contemplated writing this book, I thought I would knock it over in about four months working on it part time. I experimented with a short e-book first and soon found that much more time would be required — not just for the writing, but also the tables, charts, spreadsheets and diagrams, plus research on copyright, design and publishing. And that was not allowing anything for the crucial element: thinking time.

In the end, I scheduled the task for a chapter a week. That's what the average turned out to be, but the activity in that year was not in a straight line. Some weeks I was full of authorial energy; others slipped by with virtually no productivity at all. But my timeline had been realistic. I had allowed for the interruptions of other commitments and had set aside contingency time for when I might just get stuck. Which I did, several times.

Get money in

Take the same approach with money. What can you actually achieve with the amount you have? Maybe you need to streamline your ambition. Remember Ockham's razor and the 80:20 rule in chapter 9. What is the shortest and simplest route to get to the first goal? What 20 per cent of the effort gives the most result? Given that cash flow is likely to determine your success or failure, you need to use your most productive efforts to get money in as soon as possible. Be mindful that most success stories tell of *building* businesses rather than just creating them in an instant.

Reduce the amount going out

Working with a limited budget also introduces the notion of the 'asset parsimony strategy'. This was first articulated by Harvard professor Ian MacMillan, and has been developed by others since. There is nothing flash here. Parsimony is a word we associated earlier with William of Ockham. Basically this strategy is to do as much as possible with the fewest resources at the least cost.

For those prepared to make the effort, there are some free resources available, and certainly many less expensive alternatives. Your business might require a vehicle, but a new one will lose 25 per cent of its value the moment you drive out of the dealership. Buy a secondhand one instead, or lease it. Look on eBay to find a vast range of resources that can be secured for often giveaway prices.

The internet itself is a source of free resources that weren't available only a few years ago. Anybody can now make a first-phase website in a few hours using free design software. You can cut communication costs with Skype. You don't need an office if a virtual one will do. If your business fails, you won't be stuck in a long-term lease. What resources do friends and colleagues in your network have? Can you collaborate to the benefit of both parties? Make your asset strategy one of operating as close to free as possible.

Properly applied, this strategy can also raise cash. Firms are slow to liquidate underused or redundant assets. Yet they not only take up valuable space; they also need to be maintained or serviced. The sale of a physical asset frees up space, raises cash and eliminates maintenance costs. Even on the smallest scale, this is the case. Do you have underused assets that can be rented out during their down time for income? You have looked at what you can buy on eBay. What do you have to sell on it?

The core of the idea is to minimise costs. Use the following list to review your current business practices:

➡ Do not buy new what you can buy secondhand.
➡ Do not buy what you can lease.
➡ Do not lease what you can barter.
➡ Do not barter what you can borrow.

☞ Do not borrow what you can salvage.

☞ Do not salvage what you can get for free.

☞ Do not take for free what someone will pay you for taking.

☞ Do not take payment for something that people will bid for.

PART V

Recharge your marketing

Beginning with a review of your own value proposition, this section works through a financial audit of your marketing activities. Using measures based on the ROI of your marketing, you will identify the most cost-effective means of getting your message across. You will explore strategies for building repeat customers, using the internet effectively and managing your products through their own unique life cycles. Image, look and feel are all crucial to establishing a powerful marketing position, but so is the way you spend your marketing dollar. 'Recharge your marketing' puts your promotional efforts in clear financial perspective.

44

Show me the money

Check your marketing ROI before, and after, your campaign

What's the difference between marketing and sales? Certainly they have their own characteristics. Marketing creates awareness; sales takes advantage of that awareness. Marketing is about opening up opportunities; sales is about closing them. The hard part is identifying where one starts and the other stops.

In reality they are interdependent. It is hard to make a sale when there is no marketing; and there is no point in marketing if there are no sales. To make any sense out of either, they must be seen in the context of the returns they generate. Sooner or later, marketing must lead to sales revenue.

This is an area filled with hype—often for good reason—but you have to apply some financial measures. This is not about sending the fun police into the exciting marketing division, but it does mean that sales and marketing need to be financially accountable.

Theory and reality

Most business principles address quantities. Managing cash flow means working with hard numbers. Making a financial decision requires real data. Even team performance can be assessed against numerical goals.

Marketing presents more of a problem. It can be difficult enough to measure the impact of a marketing event on revenue, let alone to forecast it ahead of the campaign. Large corporations with professional marketing departments struggle with this. Smaller firms suffer from a lack of customer data and therefore tend to use methods that apply only to their current situation.

To make commercial marketing sense, you have to combine accepted theory with reality. The theory has been around for some time. Most of it is common sense and you will examine it in this section. Meanwhile, the emergence of the internet as a core marketing tool has introduced some new realities. The internet produces a huge amount of data and as a result there is more mathematics in marketing. Look, for example, at the impact of 'search engine optimisation' (SEO).

SEO and SEM

If you don't know what SEO is, you need to find out. But for now, this short explanation covers the basics. In your website, certain words or phrases are nominated as 'metatags'. These are the words the search engine looks for before listing your site on its results pages. For example, if you sell flowers on the internet, you would tag words such as 'flowers', 'bouquets', 'birthday presents', 'floral gifts', 'roses', 'florist' and so on. If a potential buyer searches 'floral gifts', the engine picks up your tagged site and lists it in the results. The hard part is getting onto the first page of results. This can happen organically over time if your site is regularly referenced. Optimising your tags helps get you there more quickly.

Recognising this, the engine operators offer information about what words are generating the most searches. This is a key element in 'search engine marketing' (SEM). With Google AdWords, for example, you can search the words you think are most appropriate to your site. You then bid for them so that a simple ad for your services will appear on the results page. In our example, you could pay a fee to have a small ad turn up on the first page of results every time someone searches 'floral gifts'. These are the ads on the top and/or right-hand side of a Google results page. You might lodge $100 with Google, and this is drawn down when your ad is shown, subject to the cost of the term 'floral gifts'. The bid price might be $1 per hit. More popular words may have higher prices and less popular ones lower prices.

The important part is that you can monitor your effectiveness. You will know:

▷ how many people have seen your results listing
▷ how many have looked at your ad
▷ how many have clicked through to your site
▷ which words are working best for you.

This is the basic form of SEM. However, it is a subject in its own right. You need to become fully acquainted with it if you are not already, or appoint someone to manage it.

For the purposes of this chapter, however, SEM shows just how powerful data-driven marketing can be. Because internet marketing is still in its infancy, no-one has really worked out how to price some of these models. The AdWords bidding system sets a market price for key words, but in my experience, clear logic is yet to emerge in pricing. However, the fact that there are bids at all means that market forces are recognising its power.

This begins to put some real data into the analysis of marketing activities for even the smallest operator. Compare SEM with placing an ad in your local paper or organising a spot on radio. It can give you feedback on just how many people have actually looked at your website or ad, or clicked through to it from some other source, and what that source is. This, in turn, puts huge pressure on other forms of media to demonstrate their effectiveness. It also motivates business to focus more clearly on the commercial sense of their overall marketing spend. For you, it means being very clear about the outcome you want to achieve, and then matching that with the relevant advertising format, whether it be on the internet or on billboards.

Matching the cost of revenue

Building on the internet's functionality is the easily monitored 'click-through-to-sale'. In this case, you pay for an internet ad only when someone has clicked through from your ad onto your site and has actually made a purchase. The cost of such a click-through is a clear cost of sale, or, alternatively, the cost of buying that customer via the campaign. With a hard number like this to work with, you can make a more sensible estimate of what it will cost to add, say, another 1000 customers.

This brings us back to measured goals. How do you make marketing decisions that help you achieve your mission? If the aim is to optimise returns, how do you know your marketing efforts are generating a positive return on investment (ROI)?

Knowing just how much you need to spend to secure another sale, or another customer, is one thing. But before you can do that, you need to know just how much that extra sale is going to contribute to the mission—not simply how much revenue it generates, but how much actual profit it will contribute. Even in the case of the click-through-to-sale (where you know the actual cost of the promotion), you still need to know that the cost is less than the net contribution to earnings.

Take the following example. Say the cost of the click-through promotion is $200 per sale. Your product sells for $1000 and your profit margin is 15 per cent—that is, $150. In this case, the click-through promotion is reducing your net earnings by $50 every time a customer takes up the offer. For every $200 you pay for the sale, you are only getting back $150. However, if the profit margin is 25 per cent ($250), each additional sale adds $50 to the bottom line.

So the starting point for constructing a marketing campaign needs to be an examination of the profit margin on the product you are promoting.

How much do you have to spend?

First of all, ignore fixed costs. That's because they are, after all, fixed. You will incur these no matter what. In fact, the whole point of the campaign may be to generate more volume from your fixed expenditure, like the capital you have tied up in land and buildings. One more sale won't affect those costs; it will just increase the return on them.

What you do need to calculate is the *variable* cost of producing an additional item. These are the input costs, transport charges, handling fees or employment and other expenses that will be required to deliver that extra unit.

Add these up and deduct the total from the sale price of the unit. That will give your 'variable profit margin' (VPM) on the additional sale. This is how much money you have available to spend on promotions to attract that extra sale without losing money. If you spend it all, the campaign breaks even. Spend more, and the campaign is a net loss. Spend less, and the campaign contributes to profitability.

From there you can easily work out the ROI of your marketing investment. For example, a click-through campaign with a variable cost per unit of $750 and a sale price of $1000 would have a VPM per unit of $250—that is, a margin of 25 per cent. You could spend up to that amount on buying a customer and still break even.

The cost of the click-through promotion was $200 per sale, which leaves an ROI of $50. If the campaign achieved sales of 1000 units, the total return would be $50 000, after paying the provider of the click-through campaign a total of $200 000.

This example makes it all look easy to quantify. Not every marketing model is as straightforward as a click-through campaign. Nor are such campaigns suitable for every type of product or service. Nonetheless, the equation for working out the ROI doesn't change. It's the same regardless of the media used or the model that is applied. It can be simply expressed in the following equation:

$$\text{ROI} = \frac{\text{VPM} \times \text{additional sales} - \text{cost of campaign}}{\text{cost of campaign}}$$

Or, using the numbers in our example:

$$\text{ROI} = \frac{\$250 \times 1000 - \$200\,000}{\$200\,000}$$

$$= \frac{\$50\,000}{\$200\,000}$$

$$= 25 \text{ per cent}$$

This summarises the things we need to know when assessing whether or not a particular marketing exercise will contribute to the mission. They are:

▷ the VPM
▷ the number of additional sales
▷ the cost of the campaign.

The first one is relatively easy to work out. The other two are unknowns until the results are in. At the planning stage, they will be forecasts only. But by working out your VPM ahead of a marketing project, you will be able to estimate your performance. It will put your plans into a financial context before you go ahead.

Just as important, however, is the need to analyse the results after the campaign.

Before and after

Always keep track of your successes and failures. Build up a history of what works, what doesn't, and why. You don't need a large marketing department to do this. Some campaigns are very straightforward. Small businesses can use simple promotions that are easily monitored. A letterbox drop in which the customer receives a discount coupon enables shopkeepers to compare the response with the cost of the drop. Collating such results is just one way of building up a profile of what works for the local demographic.

Similarly, loyalty cards such as 'Get the 10th coffee free' are simple to cost and monitor. That assessment still draws on the same equation. The cost is the implicit 10 per cent discount, the number of sales generated by the system is clear, and the shop would have worked out the VPM before it set the discount. It will only be worth doing if the net contribution is greater than the cost of the campaign.

It's getting easier and harder

The growing availability of good data has levelled the playing field in some sectors. Smaller businesses now have access to information that used to be collected only by those who could afford the research. Take TrueLocal. It is essentially the classifieds reinvented, where the traditional local press offers small businesses an online opportunity to market themselves and monitor the results.

TrueLocal itself does the national advertising of the service. Users can tailor marketing to their target locality and, as for Google AdWords, they can pay a premium to climb the rankings of the results page. Working back from the results, it is not hard to analyse your ROI. It is simply a matter of subtracting the cost of the listing from the revenue gained from new customers who contacted you through TrueLocal, then dividing the answer by the cost of the listing.

The bad news is that, over time, more of your competitors will be doing it.

Oddly, determining ROI can often be more difficult with sophisticated media such as television, because the connection between the spend and the result is less quantifiable.

Ratings give some guidance on how many people probably saw your commercial. You can often include diagnostics in your sale documentation, such as asking customers where they heard about the offer. Some distribution channels provide monitoring services so that you can obtain clear data from the process. Getting real precision, however, is not easy.

Whatever process you use, monitor the results and build up a clear picture of what works and what doesn't. This can be frustrating, but you should never lose sight of the fact that the ROI of your marketing efforts is the only way you can relate it to the mission of your business.

Try this

The application of ROI to marketing might appear daunting, but you can take the first step now—measure the VPM of a product or service you want to promote. It will let you know how much you can spend. This is the beginning of targeting just what you want to achieve with a marketing campaign. Only when you know how much you have available to spend can you determine the most profitable way of achieving a return from your efforts.

More marketing assessment

In the next few chapters, we will look at broader issues around marketing and at some of the well-tested tools for developing and assessing any promotional idea, be it a letterbox drop or a national television campaign. ROI, however, will remain a determining factor when making decisions. It is a constant in marketing management. Any business investment in time, money and people is required to meet certain return criteria. Marketing is no different. It has to face the same music as the rest of the firm.

The marketing mix
Understand the basic tools

Marketing is a science in itself. There is an entire toolkit of processes to help you determine the best practice for your product or service. We will look at several in the following chapters. They are not set formulas and need to be used creatively, but they will help you decide where you should focus your efforts. They include:

▷ the unique selling proposition (USP)
▷ the principles of branding
▷ the four P's of marketing
▷ the marketing funnel
▷ the product life cycle.

The USP

This well-worked idea is still remarkably useful. Its function is to give you a clear focus on what it is you are selling. It may be a product, a service, an idea, a solution or even a feeling. Variations on the theme include 'unique value propositions' (which emphasise the values underlying your business) and 'unique emotional propositions' (which focus on the efficiency, freedom or peace that your products deliver). There is also the 'tribal selling proposition', which relates your market niche to your way of life and those who share it.

Whatever you call it, a USP must differentiate you from your opposition. It does not necessarily mean that you must have the best product or service. But it does mean that you have a key strength you believe a client will value, and that you believe you can deliver at all times. It might simply be a convenient location.

Your USP

Table 45.1 provides a template in which you can list the key selling propositions that are unique to you. What is it about you personally, or your business, that is special? For example, are you fast, prompt, thorough, punctual, responsive, presentable, diligent, flexible, multiskilled, reliable, friendly, experienced or businesslike?

Table 45.1: template for key selling propositions

	Your firm	Small competitor	Medium-sized competitor	Large competitor
Unique attributes				
Customer satisfaction				
Look and feel				
Product				
Service				
Other attributes				

If you are someone who always meets deadlines, don't hold back. Make it clear that your service and product are highly dependable. The international courier FedEx reinforces its reliability via a clearly stated USP: 'When your package absolutely, positively has to get there overnight'.

You can see plenty of examples of key selling propositions around you in daily life. You may not like McDonald's food, but might appreciate the sheer consistency of their product offering. It is always the same wherever you go, and you can depend on them to serve you in a short space of time. It is not only fast food; it is also convenient food. Like many franchises, a key factor is the simplicity of the offering.

Think about what your product provides in terms of customer satisfaction. This is different from thinking about your physical product. Focus on your customer's needs and feelings. People buy goods and services to find a solution—something that makes them feel comfortable with the result. What problem or need can your solution address? Exactly what problem do you solve? How does the customer feel when you achieve that?

You must make your USP appeal to the client at an emotional level. This is fundamental to a USP that works. Advertisements for shavers talk less about the quality of the blade and more about the feel of the blade gliding smoothly over the skin. Gillette appeals to the male ego: 'The best a man can get'. What is the 'look and feel' of your product or service? What is the experience you want to share with your customers?

Think about your actual product. Identify a feature or capability that is unique or superior to the competition—something that allows you to confidently say: 'No, we don't do that. What we focus on is…' Remember that there is not much business sense in focusing on quality if what the market wants is quantity.

Similarly, a complicated service may be a less effective solution than a promptly delivered simple service. The famous Avis line 'We try harder' clearly acknowledged that Avis weren't number one. Originally, it read 'We're number two; we try harder'. Eventually, their success led them to drop the first half of this slogan.

Lastly, look at your service. How easy is it to buy your product? Do customers come back because they like the service? Why? What is it about you, your people and your product that brings them back or encourages them to buy more from you than they do from your competitors?

Say exactly what you are

Your USP may be a simple statement that focuses on that one thing that works to your advantage. Alternatively, it can incorporate a number of elements that appeal to the customer. Take Domino's Pizza: 'You get fresh, hot pizza delivered to your door in 30 minutes or less — or it's free'. Not much missing there. Coca-Cola is by most measures one of the strongest brands in the world. Its USP is one of the simplest, yet it does not focus on any particular quality of the product. It focuses on the product's uniqueness: 'It's the real thing'.

Compare key selling propositions

When you have finished listing your own attributes, look at three competitors, preferably one large, one medium-sized and one small. This will help you look beyond the obvious and will clarify the advantages of different-sized enterprises. What are the key propositions that they are selling? Examine them in the same areas — their customer satisfaction, their 'feel', their product and their service. List these in the table.

Now rank yourself and the three competitors from 1 to 10 in all the areas you have listed. Look for where you have an advantage over any of the competition. Are you able to attract business away from some of the larger players due to your size or flexibility? Are there aspects of your product where you have a natural advantage that you can develop more aggressively? This process will draw attention to attributes you may not have known you had. At the same time, it will focus on the strengths of the competition and how you might combat these.

What is your USP?

Once you have a clear ranking and a total score for each firm, narrow down your key advantages and work them into a simple tag line that emphasises your strengths. This is your USP. Write it on a piece of paper and stick it on the wall. Think about it over the next few days. Run it by colleagues or customers or suppliers. Over time, it will evolve into a strong statement—based on your strengths—of where you position yourself in the market. As such, it will be a core reference point in your marketing decisions. Use it to ask if a new marketing initiative really drives home what you are good at.

Establish your brand

Create value, not just sales

'The true product of a business is the business itself' says Michael Gerber in his best-selling book *The E-Myth*. Gerber uses McDonald's as a prime example. The core physical product may be a hamburger, but when you think of McDonald's you see a much broader image of a type of business. It is the 'look and feel' of McDonald's that drives its customer loyalty. You know it will be clean. Parking will be easy. Regardless of location, all items will be exactly the same. The kids can play safely in the activity centre. It won't take long. It won't cost much. You even know what words the staff will use as you approach the counter. And if you are in a hurry, there's always the drive-through window.

This is all about 'brand image'. None of those things have much to do with hamburgers. A lot of people who don't even like hamburgers go to McDonald's. They go there because they know exactly what they will get. There is nothing 'iffy' about making that choice. I'm not a huge fan, but when my children were young, time was short and the car was full of noisy, hungry kids. McDonald's was the easiest decision to make.

That is the advantage of clear branding. It speeds up the consumer's decision making. Convenience is a major driver of choice. Having your product clearly branded makes it easier for the customer to choose your product and helps them do so quickly.

Build a brand position

If you have been conscientious in developing your USP, you are already well on the way to building your brand. Don't be put off by the sliding popularity of the term USP. Define it broadly and it will give you good insights into brand development. It will also make you aware that, in many ways, you already have a brand image, even though you have never spelt it out.

If you are comfortable that you have a well-established brand, take time now to review it. Building a brand is one thing; maintaining it is another. Either process is a key part of the platform underneath your success. A central element is its consistency—not just in the obvious things like naming and logos, but in the whole process of delivering the product. But let's start with the simple things.

Logos

Does your logo work? Do you have one? A lot of people who start a business try to be too cute with things like logos. You only have to look around to see that the strongest brands often have extremely simple logos: Apple's is an apple; Batman's is a bat; Shell's is a shell; Playboy's is a bunny with a bow tie. Some, such as Coca-Cola, IBM and David Jones, are simply typographical.

Naming

Similar rules apply to naming. Keep it simple. Apply it consistently. Apply it constantly. Develop your own style guide and stick to it. Use the same typeface on your letterheads, your website, your ads, your packaging and your signage. Set headings in a certain type size and subheadings in a slightly smaller one. Keep body copy the same. Display tables and charts in the same format.

Use professionals

Developing a name, logo and tag line is a process you can do yourself, but it is worthwhile spending some money to have this done professionally. Your own view of your own business, and your own view of your customers, is not the only view. It pays to get these things right at the beginning, because building a strong brand means not changing it very often, if at all.

Question the rules

There is a lot of debate about business names. Some suggest not using location-specific names for fear of curbing opportunities for future expansion into other areas. There is something to this, but a product or service that clearly establishes a strong and reliable reputation can still become a national brand. Think of Melbourne IT or Bendigo Bank.

Equally, using your own name can have limitations, but it hasn't stopped Dick Smith becoming a country-wide retail network or prevented Jim's Mowing from growing a national franchise business.

The reason these names have achieved their prominence is the consistency of their brand image. As we said at the start, it is not just the product. It's the trust in the product, the quality of the service, the people who present it, the reliability of the delivery — the overall 'look and feel' of the business.

What this means is that branding is not simply a marketing concept. If you are thinking about your branding policy only as a means to making more sales, you are missing the bigger picture. Properly executed, your brand is your business and it is central to your mission.

Create value

Success in branding is increasingly measured in financial terms. The notion of 'brand equity' is frequently used to rate the world's top brands, and it can be central to the valuation of a business.

In the 2009 Interbrand ranking of Australian companies, first place went to Telstra. The judging panel estimated that its brand alone was worth $9.7 billion, well ahead of the major banks. Three of these took second, third and fourth places: Commonwealth Bank ($7.1 billion), National Australia Bank ($5.1 billion) and Westpac ($4.8 billion). Woolworths took fifth place ($4.6 billion).

Successful branding brings significant value to any business, not just large corporations. Your brand itself, rather than the product, attracts customers and therefore value. Review your own branding policy. It should be delivering the following:

❯❯ *Easy choice.* As with the McDonald's example, branding simplifies the consumer's decision making. It is easier for them to make the decision to buy.

❯❯ *Differentiation.* Even small and subtle shifts in branding can set your product apart from all the others with a clear identity of its own.

❯❯ *Premium pricing.* Products with established brands are able to charge higher prices than unbranded goods; this will boost margins and profitability.

❯❯ *Loyalty.* If your brand is backed by consistent delivery and quality of product, consumers simply form a habit of buying your product or service. The likelihood of repeat sales is greater.

❯❯ *Distribution.* National distribution channels will be more willing to stock your product if the brand has a well-developed identity.

❯❯ *Funding.* Banks and other financiers like brands. A new initiative to expand your business will receive more favourable consideration if the brand's track record is well established.

❯❯ *Brand leveraging.* You can use an established brand to launch expansion or diversification into new markets. Virgin started with record stores, but now there are Virgin Airlines, Virgin Finance and more.

❯❯ *Brand equity.* For all of these reasons, your brand has value. Because of this, you can sell it.

This last point ties in to the long-term achievement of your business mission. You may not want to sell your business, but maintaining it in a way that maximises its worth shows that it is maximising value for the firm's shareholders. An optimised brand is clear evidence of that.

Operating advantages of clear branding

Branding strategy helps you streamline your business processes into their most efficient form. The best way to establish your brand is to ensure that all products and processes are clearly defined. This means your business process increasingly takes the form of a template. All steps — production, pricing, distribution, customer service, packaging, delivery and features — follow the same rules. You should eventually be able to use branding strategy to write a manual on how to run a business that is very brand-conscious, because this, after all, establishes the 'look and feel' across the whole enterprise.

This ensures the integrity of the business image across the entire spectrum of operations. But it also takes you, and your ego, out of the equation. You may love your business and want to run it forever, but you are mortal. What would happen to your business, your employees and your family if you were gone tomorrow?

With or without you

One way of judging your business success is to ask yourself the question, 'Is the future of the business dependent on me?' This is not simply a matter of coping with your departure from the planet. It may open up a whole new lease of life for your business thinking and your motivation.

If you have perfected a business template, you are ready to expand. Owning an enterprise that is not dependent on you is a powerful position. With the right people and right resources, you can more easily replicate the business in a different suburb, city or state—or a different country, for that matter. Nor does this have to be the hard slog of organic growth. A fully developed brand opens up the possibility of franchising, and with it, an entirely new business model.

You may not wish to pursue any of these growth strategies, but the fact you have those options will increase the value of your firm. It reinforces the earlier point: if you want to, you can sell it. And you can sell it for more. It has become an independent entity that has value in its own right.

If your long-term aim is to hand over your business to the highest bidder and retire, or pass it on to your children, or be taken over, listed or merged, you need a clear branding policy. Building on it, and maintaining it, will optimise shareholder value over the longer term, with or without you.

Organise your marketing

What, how much, where and how?

Here's another idea that has been around for a while. It remains relevant because it is a simple way of organising your marketing plans. You do so by addressing your marketing strategy around four basic headings. They each start with the letter P:

1 product
2 price
3 place
4 promotion.

Because these areas all interrelate, it is useful to work on them using a matrix like the one in figure 47.1. You need to consider each sector individually, but having them all in front of you will remind you of the specific characteristics that can promote cross-fertilisation of your plans.

Figure 47.1: a matrix for marketing plans

Product What are you actually selling?	Place What is the right distribution channel?
Price What is your pricing strategy?	Promotion How will you reach your customers?

Product

You have already looked at the unique characteristics of your product or service. In that process, you identified various marketable features together with a sense of what your customers are looking for—not just in terms of functionality, but also in terms of the problems your product solves and the emotional responses that people have to it. However, it is not enough for your product to simply have these characteristics. These features need to be clearly presented to the customer.

Examine your design and packaging. Does it match the characteristics you want to focus on? Does the 'look and feel' of the product reflect those characteristics? Are the features, in particular those that are integral to your USP, clearly spelt out to the customer?

Review the product from the buyer's perspective. What does it look like? Check the size, colour, typeface and attractiveness. Describe the function, appearance and features of other products in the sector so that you have a very clear picture of what you are specifically selling.

Use this process to critically review your product. This is an exercise in its own right. Refer also to chapter 39 for a closer examination of what is happening in the marketplace. This may suggest a repackaging project or a product relaunch, but leave that for a later date. For now, look to work with what you have.

Price

Price is the most flexible marketing tool. It can:

- be changed quickly
- be bundled with other offers
- be discounted to boost turnover
- make a statement about your quality
- be used to command a premium
- attract customers through 'loss leading'.

However, it can also cost you money.

Businesses often look only at the competition and then set their prices around them. This passive approach can work, but it's not optimal. When developing your pricing strategy, focus on what you want to achieve.

Firstly, set a price that will generate a profit, not just revenue. You saw the importance of this in chapter 44, where you looked at the ROI of marketing activities. Your price must produce a net profit margin that provides an ROI that is acceptable to your firm. The price that provides this ROI is the platform on which you will base your pricing strategy. This does not mean that you will not decide to sell your product for more or less than that price. Rather, it sets up a commercial benchmark for making those decisions.

Many small businesses set their prices too low. They often overlook their own advantages, such as convenience or flexibility, and what those features are worth. A coffee shop in a busy railway station can charge prices higher than those of its competitors only 100 metres away. A small hamper delivery firm can charge more by allowing customisation of hampers rather than offering only a fixed range. If you set your basic pricing platform too low, you have little room left for price flexibility.

Choose a pricing strategy

Having put in place your pricing parameters, you need to decide what you want to achieve. The simplest price strategy is a competitive one. That is, you know what the prevailing market price is, and that is where you will position your product. As we said, this works, but only if two other conditions are met:

1 The market is a fairly level playing field in which you expect to capture a reasonable market share at that price.
2 The market price is a profitable one for your firm.

It is likely it won't be that easy. Your product may be new and command no loyalty, or your existing product may be underperforming its potential to grow well beyond its current market share. Alternatively, you may be trying to penetrate a new market or fight off new competition in your own. You may want to boost the presence of your entire range of products. Pricing depends on what you want to achieve. Keeping in mind your ROI, examine your pricing options in terms of your marketing objectives. What is the outcome you are targeting? Consider volume, customer loyalty, product range and statement pricing.

Volume

Boosting turnover or market share via discounting has little value in its own right. Discounting prices only erodes margins and increases the likelihood of price wars. Smaller businesses usually lose price wars. Higher volume needs to be seen in the context of what that added market strength delivers. For example, will greater margin pressure arising from a discount campaign be offset by greater volume discounts from your suppliers? Can storage costs be reduced by shifting excess inventory? Is there a case for loss minimisation in closing out a slow-moving product line? Make a careful study of the ROI of such initiatives. If they make sense, apply them to your pricing decision, but treat discounting with great caution.

Customer loyalty

Discount cards, loyalty programs, warranties and the like all work to attract and keep customers. They have the advantage of maintaining your commercial pricing while generating return business, but they all have a cost. They should be regularly reviewed for their effectiveness and refreshed in terms of your customers' apparent priorities and values. Membership programs, especially those on the internet, provide opportunities for tiered pricing and the ability to make special offers to selected customers. The database arising from signed-on membership creates an asset that has value in its own right.

Product range

Is the product part of a range? Can you make the entire range attractive by offering discounts on accessories while maintaining the price on the core product? Does it make sense to bundle the entire range in specially priced packages? Can you encourage the equivalent of 'up-sizing' by splitting off certain features and offering them as options? This can help capture a wider range of customers, as it will appeal to those wanting the basic product as well as less price-sensitive clients who want the full service. Software companies increasingly use this strategy through 'versioning', where they offer different configurations of the same product.

Statement pricing

Economy pricing communicates that the product is a reliable, generic item sold at an affordable price. On the other hand, special features, sophisticated packaging and high product quality virtually demand premium pricing. Customers expect this and certain segments prefer it. Which segment is your objective? What market statement do you intend to make? What features can you add to your product to underwrite a new and higher price?

Be flexible

Pricing strategy lends itself to a fast response when required. Small businesses can implement price changes quickly, but so can many large ones. Harvey Norman, for example, can identify a trend in consumer preferences, decide on a special product promotion and have the advertising campaign running on prime-time television the following evening.

Always check the margin

Special promotions are usually more tactical than strategic, yet there is also a case for a marketing strategy that consists of a series of tactical promotions. Late night television is full of examples of strategies built around special promotions of simple products. The guiding rule for promotion via pricing, however, remains the same: know the marginal return from the extra item sold or the new customer attracted. Check your ROI and always be aware of how quickly margins are eroded. A 10 per cent increase in the price of a product can often have virtually no appreciable impact on volume, whereas discounts impact quickly on ROI. It's a key rule about margins: raising prices increases margins by more than the price increase; cutting prices reduces margins by more than the price cut.

For example, if it costs $8 to make and market a product that you sell for $10, your net profit margin is 20 per cent — that is, $2 as a percentage of $10. If you raise the price by 10 per cent to $11, your margin doesn't go up by 10 per cent. It goes up by over a third to 27 per cent and you increase your cash margin on the product by 50 per cent (from $2 to $3).

Unfortunately, the converse is also true. If you cut your price by 10 per cent to $9, your margin doesn't fall by 10 per cent. It plunges by 45 per cent to 11 per cent and your net profit halves (from $2 to $1). It's something to keep in mind.

Placing and promoting

Being seen and heard

Regardless of how good you think your product is, or how compellingly you think it is priced, it will not be successful if it is not exposed to your potential customers. They not only need to hear about it; they also need to see it.

Placing your product

'Placing' refers to how you get your product in front of the customer. Look, for example, at my father's simple strategy during the Great Depression. (He probably would not have referred to it as a strategy; he would have called it 'common sense'. This is what successful marketing is usually about.)

My father grew up in a small country town in southern New South Wales. In his teens, the depression was in full swing and the town was on its knees. He worked in the local emporium, a kind of general store that was the main retail outlet. There was no money; the business struggled and eventually closed down.

His placing idea was simple. Collaborating with a friend who had a flat-bed truck, he offered to buy the entire merchandise of the emporium on consignment. They loaded it onto the vehicle, drove across the border to a town in Victoria that had just had a successful wheat harvest and sold the lot off the back of the truck. I don't know what his margins were and I am not sure he would have worked out his ROI. But he had a keen eye for product, price and place.

He used this method to survive the depression. He travelled around the country undertaking the simplest form of business: trading. He didn't make any product. He just bought it, priced it and placed it.

Think about that. No distributors, few overheads and cash turnover. Because he was selling off the truck for cash, there were no problems with ageing receivables. And as it was on consignment, the money was in before it went out. From the point of view of working capital management, it doesn't get much better.

Financial considerations

Even today, these are the things you need to take into account when considering the financial aspect of placing your product. Choosing your distribution channel will not only depend on matching it with the market position of your product, but also with a market structure that you can afford. There will be costs attached to whatever structure you decide. Your choice will determine your margins, your overheads and the working capital environment you will be operating in.

Your choice of channel will be direct sales, indirect sales or somewhere in between (see figure 48.1).

Figure 48.1: distribution options

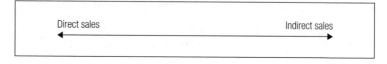

If you opt for a direct channel—that is, you manufacture the product or service, or you buy it in, and then sell it directly to the customer—you will still have the cost of setting up that channel and providing the logistics of physically delivering the product. You may build an excellent system, but it will take both time and money. Nonetheless, there will be no distributors, and payment will probably be cash or on delivery.

A faster route to the customer may well be to also sell to retailers who will effectively place your product for you. This, of course, adds another stakeholder. The discount you provide for the retailer to stock your product makes the first cut in your margin. However, they will shoulder the transaction costs of each individual sale and if a sufficient number of retailers stock your product, the higher volume may offset the reduction in your margin.

At the opposite end is a sales model based completely on indirect sales. Here, the number of stakeholders will have grown to include agents, wholesalers, retailers or logistics firms before the product finally ends up placed in front of the customers—and hopefully is sold to them. The equation that has to be optimised, however, is no different from my father's: it is the combination that maximises turnover and cash management while keeping overheads to a minimum. This aspect of making decisions about 'place' is purely a financial one.

Who do you want to place it in front of?

The other aspect is choosing the channel that is most appropriate to your objective. Does your product lend itself to intensive selling to the greatest number of people, or does it require selective selling to a target market segment? For example, is it best sold over the internet or through department stores? Or are sales optimised by promoting through a small number of quality boutiques? The answer to these questions lies in market segmentation analysis. That means simply knowing your customers: who they are, where they are, what they want and how they want to buy it.

This is not a hard process. Examine your market using the following perspectives:

ᗑ *Demographic*. Who are they? Analyse their age, gender, education, life-stage, occupation, income, social class, religion or any other characteristic. What distinguishes them?

℥ *Geographic*: Where are they? Do they live in the country or the city? Are they isolated or do they have easy access to distribution outlets? Are they in certain cities but not others? Is their environment hot, cold or temperate? Is it logistically hard to provide service to them?

℥ *Psychographic*. What do they want? Look at the lifestyle profile of your target customers. What are their values? What do they spend money on? Check the relevance of notions such as 'generation X', 'generation Y' and 'baby boomers'.

℥ *Behaviour*. How do they want to buy your product? On the internet? At the mall? By mail order? With loyalty points attached? At Christmas? Or birthdays? Or every day? How do they spend their money? Do they use credit cards, EFTPOS, hire purchase or cash?

This is a general outline of things to consider in market segmentation. You can investigate your market as far as you want. This suits the shift from 'mass-marketing' to 'mass-customisation', and on to the 'micro-marketing' that the internet has made more accessible to even the smallest business. Nonetheless, when you have carefully profiled your customer base and worked out where you need to place your product, you still need to take equal care with the financial analysis of that option to ensure you can get it there at the minimum cost and with profitable margins intact.

Promotion

Thorough market segmentation will also clarify how you need to promote your product. The supposed benefits and audiences of all advertising and promotional avenues are relatively well broadcast, if not always wholly believable. However, such information will help you make your decision.

The likely profile of your target customers will help you decide on the best way to reach them. For a small retail outlet making a special offer, this can be as simple as a mail drop into the letterboxes of homes within walking distance of the shop. At the other end of the spectrum, a national branding exercise might demand prime-time television campaigns on all free-to-air channels over a prolonged period.

There is, of course, everything in between, and there is always timing. There is seasonality in most markets, be it winter or summer fashion, or chocolate eggs at Easter. Holidays play a massive role in spending patterns, as do the usual suspects such as the state of the economy, the arrival of tax rebates and the level of interest rates. The marketing mix is never static.

Once you have formulated a strategy that is right for you, monitor it actively. Experiment with it over time and track the results. What does a price change actually achieve in terms of volume, market share or margin? What promotions always yield results? In what locations? Via what medium? At what time of the year? Have you tried all the promotional vehicles?

Keep stirring the mix. There are plenty of options. As long as you track this over time, you will identify what works best for your business. Consider this checklist of possible marketing activities:

- direct mail
- direct email
- radio advertising
- search marketing
- business directory listings
- seminars and conferences
- trade fairs and exhibitions
- advertorials
- letterbox drops
- press releases
- online newsletters

- ➲ online special promotions
- ➲ growing your sales team
- ➲ special in-store promotions
- ➲ telemarketing
- ➲ marketing alliances with complementary producers
- ➲ new brochures
- ➲ online catalogues
- ➲ mail-out of hard-copy catalogues
- ➲ relaunched websites
- ➲ local press advertising
- ➲ free offers, loyalty cards and coupon campaigns
- ➲ YouTube videos
- ➲ social media campaigns.

Weave a wider web

Make money in the free-to-free environment

What does the internet mean for business? Is it a great opportunity, or does it just mean lower prices, tighter margins and more competition?

The most remarkable thing about the web is not the explosion in what it delivers, even though just about everything can now be sourced on the web. The really remarkable thing is that so much that used to cost money is now free.

Some things have crept so quietly into our lives that we don't even think about them. Like email. Not even a trip to the post office, let alone buying an envelope or the relevant stamp. Just type and click. No overnight delivery. Just instantaneous delivery, anywhere in the world, for nothing. By the time you factor in the convenience of internet banking, the postal needs of the average business or household have shrunk by about 90 per cent.

Then there is the sheer weight of available information. After all, that is what the web was invented for: to facilitate the sharing of information. Originally it was the turf of academics searching for obscure treatises by PhD candidates in rare scholastic publications. Now anyone can search for anything, anytime, anywhere, for free.

But it's no longer just information. Products available on the web might not be free, but they are usually cheap. Downloadable products are invariably less expensive than when purchased elsewhere; auction sites provide a range of keenly priced items, both new and used. Price comparisons are easier. Some sites specialise in that alone.

What's in it for business?

All this represents opportunity and cost. The opportunities lie in harnessing the internet's natural advantages. Most of these stem from the fact that the internet is largely a free service. Properly used, it enables you to:

ᗌ expand your customer base

ᗌ boost revenues

ᗌ reduce costs

ᗌ target niche markets

ᗌ streamline transaction costs.

Australian serial entrepreneur Tim Pethick, founder of 'nudie juicies' among other things, provides an excellent example of a marketing campaign that encompasses all five of those advantages.

Tim launched a simple mobile phone that was designed specifically for children. It was called the Gecko. Apart from being cute and appealing to kids, it found favour with parents — they liked the Mum and Dad speed-dial keys, the emergency call button and special text alerts to control costs. Nonetheless, it was a specific market that required a targeted promotion.

In one experiment, Pethick trialled a traditional direct-mail campaign and a Google AdWords campaign, then compared the two.

In the direct-mail campaign, the usual set-up activities included designing and producing the relevant artwork, determining the target consumers, sourcing and renting a distribution list, engaging a distribution house, printing the mail-out and distributing it. Overall preparation time was measured in days, if not weeks.

The logistics behind the AdWords campaign were far simpler. The key words were determined, a set budget was decided and the campaign was put on the AdWords site. Clearly this was less expensive, and it was achieved in a matter of hours. These advantages alone made the web-based approach the preferred option. But the most dramatic difference came in the results. The mail-based campaign was a net loss; the web-based campaign was clearly profitable, and was more efficient by most measures, as shown in table 49.1.

Table 49.1: comparison of Gecko campaigns

Direct mail		AdWords	
Total mailed	4750	Total clicks	1735
Total cost	$9860	Total cost	$1300
Cost per unit	$2.07	Cost per click	$0.75
'Dead' letters	283 (6%)		
Response	2	Response	82
CPR	$4930	CPR	$15.85
Revenue	$290	Revenue	$11 890
Loss	$9570	Profit	$10 590

Not all comparisons would reveal such a sharp contrast. It may well be that mobile phones, as a product genre, lend themselves to internet purchases, or that this specific niche is more likely to have a preference for transacting on the web. But the results in this instance are very clear. The campaign ticks each of the five areas listed earlier as opportunities offered by the web. The customer base was expanded (82 responses versus 2). Revenues were sharply higher. Total costs were nearly 90 per cent lower. The CPR (cost per response) showed the internet targeted this niche more precisely, and in the case of the web campaign, the purchase was completed online directly by the customer, reducing transaction costs.

Getting a perspective on 'free'

Although this comparison illustrates key advantages of internet commerce, it also demonstrates how to use the opportunity. In this case, there was a clear product with a target market—that is, there was a specific purpose. There will not necessarily be a similar benefit in building an extensive web presence for its own sake. Too often, internet projects become an expense base rather than a set of tools for optimising the ROI of your marketing activities.

This raises the whole question of 'free'.

The very nature of the internet has brought about a shift in economic culture. Because the web itself is free, there is an expectation that many things that are offered on it should also be free. The disregard for copyright, music piracy, spamming and plagiarism of many web-users reflects this shift. For business, it is exacerbated by the number of products that are actually made available for free.

It is important to recognise that 'free' is not a new commercial notion. When I visit my local shopping mall, I will be offered free samples of food and other products. I will be offered free movie tickets with purchases from certain stores. After several coffees, I will be given one free. If I sign up for the loyalty card of any brand store, I will receive discounts on my current and future purchases. The department store will deliver for free once I have spent a certain amount. At the bookstore I can buy two books for the price of one, and the restaurant at which I eat will validate my parking. As I walk to the car park, I will pass many stores promoting big discount sales or special offers.

So there is nothing new about free stuff.

You will have exactly the same experience scrolling through websites. And, of course, none of it is free. It is all costed in somewhere. Whether it is a cost-of-sale or a cost-of-promotion, someone, somewhere is paying for it.

It may be fair to say that the business models applied in shopping malls are backed by a longer history of monitored results and are therefore easier to assess in terms of ROI, whereas the internet is still to some extent a black box.

Nonetheless, internet customers are now a market segment in their own right. The growth in their numbers remains phenomenal. For that reason, the results of web-based campaigns are volatile and hard to predict. There are generalised evaluations for older forms of promotion, but the measures for evaluating internet campaigns are still in a state of flux. A response rate of 2 per cent to a direct-mail campaign is considered successful, but no such 'rule of thumb' is yet clear for the web. In any case, as with the Gecko example, determining the ROI is as much a result of the low cost of implementation as it is a function of the response rate.

Some successes have no staying power

Many of the high-profile web-based successes are wild cards that have emerged from testing the frontier of 'free'. They may show the way, but they are often not easily repeatable.

Take the rock group Nine Inch Nails. Led by Trent Reznor, this industrial rock band launched a series of four albums (*Ghosts I–IV*) in 2008. The first album in the series was offered free as an internet download. Also, using a Creative Commons licence (a less-restrictive form of copyright developed specifically for the internet), all four albums were made available on a slightly more limited basis.

Despite this apparent commercial suicide, the series went on to be the highest-selling product on Amazon's MP3 store in 2008. Additional revenue came from limited editions and extras such as Blu-ray discs. Not a bad result. And one in which Reznor's margins were far greater than the usual rock band returns, as no traditional record company was involved. Most of the income went directly to Nine Inch Nails.

But there have been few similarly spectacular examples since. As with any innovative marketing, the early adopters receive great publicity and often good results. But they are soon imitated, and the results become more volatile and the margins narrower. Such experiments now take place daily on the web. Put the word 'free' in front of any word and search it. Enough said.

Marketing basics

Keep a perspective on this by remembering marketing basics: what do you want to achieve and what is the ROI of the exercise? This can be costed in exactly the same way that businesses in the shopping mall approach their own 'free' promotions. The rules don't change just because it's the internet.

The range of promotional strategies that apply to traditional marketing also apply to the web, and with the same conditions. At what price point does free delivery make sense? What happens to margins when something is offered for free? What is the cost of that extra sale or customer? What can you afford to spend—that is, give away—to achieve the result you want?

In working through this process, visit an established marketing concept: the marketing funnel (see figure 49.1). It will help you align what you have to do with what you want to achieve.

The marketing funnel does exactly what it says. It outlines the marketing steps that lead ultimately to a transaction. Each requires a different, if complementary, strategy:

1 Create or expand awareness of your product or service. In the case of the web, this involves strategies to increase the number of hits on your site.
2 Once potential customers are aware, grow the importance of your product in their minds. That is, you want

customers to put your product on the list of the products they are considering.

3 Aim at making your product their preference.
4 Implement strategies that encourage customers to take action—that is, close the sale.

Figure 49.1: the marketing funnel

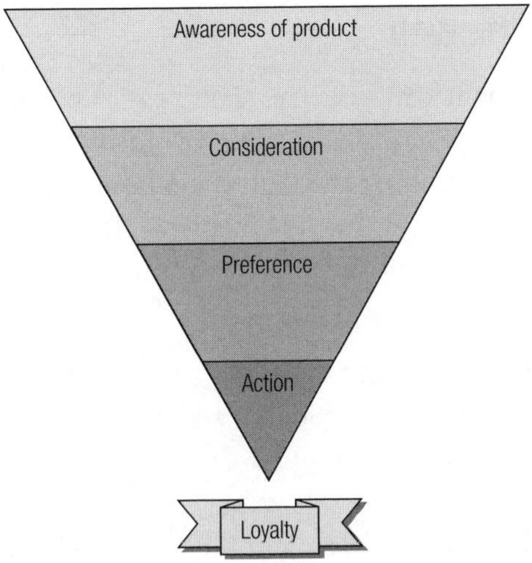

Use the web at each stage

The web offers opportunities to boost your impact at each stage. Social networking campaigns can bolster awareness. Customer rankings of your product can affect consideration. Driving home key features develops customer preferences. An attractive call to action on the web, coupled with special offers or discounts, can clinch the deal. Simple transaction options prompt the decision to purchase. Ordering and paying by 'point-and-click' is an extremely convenient way to shop.

The idea behind the funnel is to take your product into the broader marketplace and create awareness, then to manage the process all the way through to prompting the customer to act. The simpler and more convenient you make it, the more likely it is it that it will succeed. The web is very good for that.

Increasingly, marketers look to build on this process by maintaining customer loyalty via interactive web campaigns such as user-generated blogs, membership options, product chat rooms and the like.

Try using the web

What experiment can you try? The beauty of the internet is that it is not that hard (or expensive) to try something new. Spend an hour thinking through one of the following options in regard to your business. Or, better still, put one option to your think tank or set up a team to implement a web-based experiment.

⚡ *Boost hits.* Higher hit rates lead to more sales and more income opportunities. Selling advertising on your site is a function of how many people look at it. SEO addresses this, but is an art in itself. What can you offer on your site for free that will bring in the numbers? Do you have inventory of unsold product? How about a quiz with a prize, or a diagnostic test in your area of expertise?

⚡ *Develop a database.* The goal for many businesses is to build a database of customers who have consented to receive marketing information. You can legally send these customers newsletters, special offers or updates. What can you do to convince them to sign up? Can you provide free samples of your best offering in snippet form (for example, a free chapter of a book or a track from an album)? Do you already have an extensive database that can be used as a distribution channel for other products? Would an alliance with a complementary business leverage your position through joint marketing?

⋙ *Promote a product range.* You could try 'buy one and get a discount on the others' and the inevitable 'buy one, get one free'. Do you have downloadable product that can be offered at a discount?

⋙ *Maintain loyalty.* Can you build membership and loyalty by sponsoring chat rooms in your product area, or free help services? Do you have a common theme or passion around which you can create an online social network?

Whatever you decide to do, remember that the 'free' element is no different from what you give away to gain customers in the non-web sector. Cost it accordingly. Check your variable profit margin. How much can you afford to spend to get that extra sale or that extra customer? That's also how much you can afford to give away for free—either in the mall or on the internet.

PART VI

Staying recharged

Now that you have recharged your business, how will you keep it evolving? You need to sustain a refreshing approach to management. The recharged firm maintains momentum and constantly adapts to remain at the leading edge of its business environment. These closing chapters help you put in place management practices that will keep you on the front foot. Tools for assessing new strategies are explained. There are processes to help you review what this book has covered. They prompt ongoing actions that incorporate key concepts you have explored; they will help you collaborate, adapt, simplify and, ultimately, take action.

50 Look at the big picture
Use the strategy toolkit

What if you climbed the ladder to success only to find it was leaning against the wrong wall? Stephen Covey asked this question in *The 7 Habits of Highly Effective People*. Covey was talking about personal aspirations, but this question can also test your strategic thinking in business. What is the point of becoming the best provider of a product that fewer people want? Smith Corona was a well-managed company that made excellent typewriters for decades. They were still making excellent typewriters when I bought my first word processor. I never bought a typewriter again. Smith Corona's main business today is the supply of accessories for competitors' machines.

Your product may have a use-by date, but so does your strategic plan. It starts ticking the day it's created. The wall your ladder is leaning against may shift at any given moment. Styles change and people start wanting to climb a different wall. Technology can eliminate a barrier to entry in the blink of an eye. Suddenly your wall has collapsed, your ladder has crashed and so has your business. It may not be that dramatic, but in the area of strategy, there is a strong case for eternal vigilance.

For all those reasons, strategic planning is a series of sprints along different paths rather than a marathon race down a single road. Staying recharged requires constant review of the business landscape. This does not mean that you operate in a planning void where everything is constantly in a state of flux. Rather, it means that you allocate time to question the overall strategy of your business, that you do not do this alone and that you do it in a structured manner.

Build better perspective

There are a lot of strategic tools, but none fits all businesses. We touched on some in earlier chapters—templates for competitive positioning, SWOT analysis, marketing matrixes. None of these are cure-alls. They are tools, not solutions. They bring perspective and clarity to the strategic dialogue.

The product–market growth matrix

A matrix is at least two-dimensional, so there is a chance that using it will reveal at least two perspectives. Consider the 'product–market growth matrix' developed by the mathematician Igor Ansoff. This is a simple planning tool. It has limited practical use, but it clearly highlights the strategic options and risks for a firm looking to expand.

The Ansoff matrix organises the core components of existing or future strategies by the two dimensions market and product. It allows you to focus on two questions:

1 Does the firm grow by introducing new products or by building on existing ones?
2 Does it do so by penetrating more deeply into existing markets, or by expanding into new ones?

In figure 50.1 (overleaf), we have added the third dimension of risk.

Locating your strategy on the matrix identifies your options and indicates their relative risk. Activities in each quadrant raise their own specific issues.

Market development

This involves growing the market for existing products and services by, for example, shifting into new geographic areas, rebranding, implementing aggressive pricing policies or setting up new distribution channels. This is a medium-risk strategy and is often essential for maintaining competitive position as much as for generating growth.

Figure 50.1: the product–market growth matrix

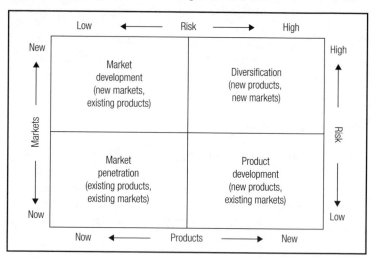

Market penetration

This is the least risky option and relies on having an established market share or position. It acknowledges that market growth is relatively static and that growth will only come through gaining market share. It is very much a 'more of the same' strategy. It is low risk, but also brings low growth and most likely, low margins.

Product development

This strategy introduces new or differentiated products into existing markets. There is a stronger element of risk, but this is offset by the use and knowledge of existing marketing and distribution channels.

Diversification

This is clearly the most risky strategy, yet there are many examples of its success. General Electric began as a turbine manufacturer, but its leasing activities grew into a major financial services business. This strategy demands exceptionally thorough and honest appraisal combined with extremely diligent execution.

Experiment with different tools

Although the product–market growth matrix does not lead you to a strategic decision, it provides a framework in which to assess the appeal and the risk of the opportunities available to you. This is the case with most matrices. Even the simple SWOT analysis, which you have used in developing both personal and team perspectives, is extremely useful when applied to the business as a whole.

PEST analysis

PEST analysis, although not a matrix in the true sense of the word, is often presented as such. Again, it will help structure your strategic considerations, not solve them. It stands for 'politics', 'economics', 'society' and 'technology'. Add-ons in recent years have seen the acronym topped and tailed with 'physical environment' and 'trade' to give PPESTT. The process drives you to review the likely trends in each area and to look at their impact on your business. Some possible trends are given in the following list:

▷ *Physical environment.* Environmental trends could be shifts in land usage or availability.
▷ *Politics.* Political trends include a change of government and a change of zoning for your business.
▷ *Economics.* Economic trends include the likely direction of the economic cycle.
▷ *Society.* Social trends include shifts in values and fashions as well as cultural differences (for example, in new locations).
▷ *Technology.* Trends in technology include developments that can affect your internal structures or your external markets.

⌦ *Trade.* These trends include globalisation, international competition and trade barriers.

Strategy cannot make sense if it does not acknowledge key trends in the marketplace and their likely impact on the firm's business.

The Boston matrix

The legendary 'Boston matrix' was originally designed by the Boston Consulting Group. It has taken a fair amount of criticism over the years, and rightly so in some areas. However, most of those who criticised the matrix were expecting it to generate a strategic silver bullet, or simply took it at face value and failed to use it creatively. Like other tools, the Boston matrix is the *starting* point for a strategic discussion, not a formula that will provide a final decision.

The Boston matrix asks you to assess each business unit or product line in terms of:

1 its position in the market
2 the outlook for the market it is in.

In other words, it uses market share and market growth. Depending on where an item sits in the matrix, it is called in somewhat colourful language a 'dog', a 'cash cow', a 'star' or a 'problem child'. These categories are shown in figure 50.2.

The Boston matrix is simplistic, but the classification raises strategic issues. A cash cow, by definition, is a mature but profitable product. Its market may not be growing, but its share is well established. It is a candidate for a 'harvest' strategy: minimise ongoing investment, maximise profits, and channel resulting cash flow into problem children or stars, which are products that have greater potential for growth in market share. Dogs are business lines where both existing share and potential growth are limited. They may be prime candidates for disposal. Problem children, also known as 'question marks', are often exciting products or services in their own right. But, like many creative teenagers, they need clear direction, specific goals and a structured plan if they are to justify investment in their potential.

Figure 50.2: the Boston matrix

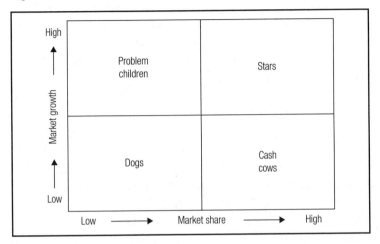

The longevity of the Boston matrix reflects the fact that it encourages strategists to look forward. Managers examining business units in each quadrant have to take a view on the future of those units

Change for change's sake

A problem with most of these tools is that they may not easily accommodate the dramatic shifts that technology and social change bring about in today's business environment. Most strategic analysis focuses on how to compete in a defined and existing marketplace. Yet many of the newest and most successful businesses have emerged in markets that didn't exist several years ago. Think of Google, Amazon or YouTube. For that matter, many businesses have simply broken away from the pack not by competing head-to-head with rivals but by discovering new, uncontested market space.

The blue ocean strategy

INSEAD academics W Chan Kim and Renée Mauborgne made this observation in developing the 'blue ocean strategy'. For their model, the preoccupation with the competition constrains businesses so that they grow only within the limitations of their existing market space, the 'red ocean', in which competitors constantly attack each other.

In the blue ocean, businesses switch their attention to alternatives rather than competitors—even to non-customers rather than customers. A good example is the increasingly popular 'Gold Class' movie theatre. Not long ago, consumers were faced with clear alternatives in this sector: spend a few hours in a restaurant or in a bar or seeing a movie. In Gold Class, customers who might have chosen only one of the alternatives can now do all three at the same time. Gold Class effectively created a new market, turning potential non-customers into premium customers. Kim and Mauborgne offer other inspired examples: *Cirque du Soleil* breaking out of the traditional circus mould and into an entirely new demographic; Borders combining coffee shops with bookshops; Swatch aligning function with fashion.

Using Kim and Mauborgne's process, you begin with a 'strategy canvas' of where a product sits in the market. List the factors of the product and market (such as price, product complexity, convenience, prestige, reputation, range and advertising spend) along a horizontal axis. Then plot the product's position against the industry standards indicated on the vertical axis.

Now look to *reduce* factors that are below industry standards, and in some cases to *eliminate* them; this will simplify your product and reduce costs. At the same time, *create* new factors to enhance your product and *raise* your offering above industry standards for other factors to make your product stand out in the marketplace.

A strategy canvas for Gold Class might look something like the chart in figure 50.3. The traditional movie theatre will likely be competitively priced. Food is provided through concessions. There is no wait service and there are no alcoholic beverages. The theatre is reasonably comfortable and is designed for an experience that represents value for money.

Gold Class, on the other hand, charges a premium price and has no concessions but introduces a food and beverage wait service including alcoholic beverages in more comfortable surroundings to provide a premier experience.

Figure 50.3: a strategy canvas for Gold Class

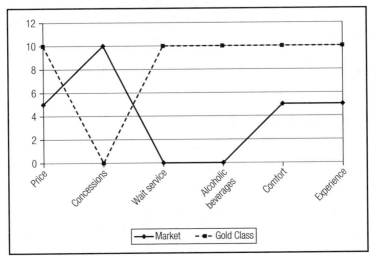

The challenge in creating a strategy canvas is to identify all the factors that make up the industry standard for your product. There are often more than you think, and often the ones that drive customers' decisions are contrary to conventional wisdom.

An example of the process in practice is Australian winemaker Casella Wines. They dramatically lifted their share of the US market by reducing or eliminating traditional market factors for wine (such as ageing quality, above-the-line marketing, wine complexity and range). Instead they focused on a simple selection of easily drinkable reds and whites in identical bottles with mid-range pricing and branding that evoked fun and adventure. The result was an offering that appealed to a much wider segment of the market. Those who were previously non-wine drinkers began buying the Casella product.

Grow your own

Tools like these are all great starting points for strategic discussion. Alternatively, you can make your own matrix. Many issues can be simply and creatively presented in this format, which brings a clear perspective to decision making. For example, you could apply Pareto's 80:20 rule to decide which action or project will get the fastest result from the least effort. Use the horizontal axis for 'impact' and the vertical axis for 'effort', as shown in figure 50.4.

Figure 50.4: an 80:20 matrix

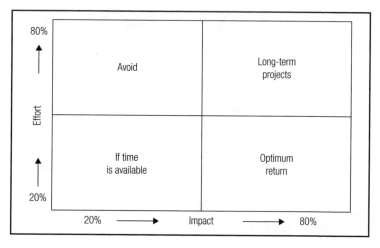

The top left quadrant includes actions that are probably not worth the effort. The optimum use of resources is in the lower right quadrant. Actions in other quadrants are not ruled out, but will either require much greater planning (such as long-term projects) or make sense only if time allows.

Begin now

Draw up a list of issues that your business is facing and examine them from different perspectives using a matrix. Try those outlined in this chapter, or add your own or others, such as expense vs revenue, time vs return, competitive strength vs market potential, or whatever is appropriate for the alternatives you are considering.

This process is part of your ongoing responsibility, not something to be left to the annual conference. Stay current with shifts in the environment. Schedule regular meetings of your strategic think tank. Use structured tools as a basis for debate and maintain the dialogue. But be careful not to let the process take on a life of its own. It is too easy to let the big questions swamp the perpetual motion generated by constant action. The active manager we defined in chapter 1 can make crucial contributions to the strategic debate, but needs to do so without neglecting other areas. Maintaining a culture of change is an important part of the manager's job, but so are the other parts.

In the next two chapters, we will look at simple processes for sustaining innovative management and business.

51 Put it all together

Stay in perpetual motion

Do you ever find yourself wanting change just for the sake of it? I almost always drive home the same way from the office. It's the quickest route. I know how to drive it: I know where the speed cameras are; I know when to be in what lane; I know how long certain traffic lights stay red. It takes about 40 minutes.

There is also a longer way. Maybe an extra 10 minutes. There are times when I just want to go home that way. There's no real reason. It is a nicer drive, but basically I am just bored with the usual route. I'd like to say that this has turned out to be my road to Damascus, but nothing particularly inspiring has ever happened when I have taken the longer way. There have been some small benefits. I discovered cheaper petrol along that route, and it takes me past a shopping centre with outlets that I would not otherwise use and that sell some things I find useful. But by and large, I just enjoy doing the drive home differently. Like a lot of us, I am someone who likes change.

A lot of us, however, don't. It is good that these people are around because they provide us with a reality check. I can be a hero at anything for a reasonable amount of time, but eventually routine gets to me. Even though nothing is broken and nothing needs fixing, I want to try doing it slightly differently. This is also good. But I need to run it past people who fully understand and appreciate the value of routine: it gets things done with the minimum of fuss.

The flip side is that routine can be stagnant. Your business will not stay at the leading edge if you are never near the edge. Putting off change puts you dangerously on track for inertia. Imbalances build up inside your business, silos form, and your organisation less and less reflects market realities. By the time you realise what has happened, it can only be reversed by major shifts in structure and policy. The people who don't like change don't like this at all.

Change versus balance

There is, of course, a middle ground—one in which change is embraced, but not at such a rapid rate that it is constantly unsettling for those who struggle with it. At the same time, it must be maintained at a speed that encourages those who are motivated by it. The middle ground is not about wholesale shifts. It's about a culture of change that regularly questions the status quo but doesn't make change for change's sake.

That is why the focus of this book is managers—those who work at the coalface to make things happen. It's about a recharge, not a rebuild. Recharging a business takes action, not talkfests. The most immediate gain in business momentum comes from taking simple steps that can be easily implemented. That alone inspires and motivates both the managers and the managed.

Any activity is like that. It chips away at inertia. A policy of constant action opens a business to new ideas and generates enthusiasm for them. The simpler the idea the better, because simple actions are easily understood and quickly put in place. That is part of a strategy for staying recharged. It breeds a culture of change that is not overwhelming. It just means that nothing is set in concrete—that new ideas are always welcomed; that they are assessed positively; and that if they make sense, they are implemented.

The business balance assessment

You have now walked through all the key dimensions of management. You have taken some action along the way and have put in place practices that increase the opportunities for perpetual motion. To some extent, you have already developed a strategy for staying recharged.

To take this to the next stage, you will undertake a short process. You already did this in chapter 2, but you need to revisit it now in light of what you have covered so far. The original aim was to prompt action in your own management style — to make sure you were good at managing yourself, so that you in turn were going to be good at managing people.

Now you need to review your business in the same way, using what you have learned. The process in chapter 2 was called a 'personal balance assessment'; you now need to do a 'business balance assessment'.

The following sections ask a lot of questions. Don't be overwhelmed by them. You don't have to answer them. Don't write anything down. Simply use them to review what we have covered in this book.

Yourself

⊅ Do you have a clear idea of what your role is?
⊅ Do you now commit time to focus on how you will carry out that role?
⊅ Have you isolated your strengths?
⊅ Are you spending more time on using them?
⊅ Have you delegated some of your weaknesses?
⊅ Have you addressed issues you had been avoiding?
⊅ How are you handling new ones that have arisen?
⊅ Have you built a think tank?
⊅ Are you taking more opportunities to collaborate with others?
⊅ Are you promoting yourself as an expert in your areas of strength?
⊅ Do you schedule time regularly to clear your desk, reboot and think?

Your finances

- ⇨ Do you now regularly review your working capital management?
- ⇨ Have you cleared away asset clutter and created a lean business?
- ⇨ Do you have a credit policy?
- ⇨ Is it managed?
- ⇨ Do you have a clear view of what your business is worth?
- ⇨ Do you have a target for what it should be worth?
- ⇨ Do you know what actions you will take to get there?
- ⇨ Do you now know what financing options are available to you, what they cost, and what will work best for you?

Your team

- ⇨ How is your team performing?
- ⇨ Have you started a new team?
- ⇨ How are you managing your team?
- ⇨ Is its structure and function in need of review?
- ⇨ Are you using your team effectively, delegating tasks that leave you free to focus on your strengths?
- ⇨ Are you managing difficult people and taking appropriate action to maintain team performance?

Your firm

- ⇨ How are your relations with your various stakeholders: your suppliers, shareholders, customers, employees, managers and the community?
- ⇨ Are there issues that need to be addressed, or projects that will use those relationships more effectively?
- ⇨ Are you managing your risks?
- ⇨ How do you compare with the competition?

▷ Do you need to relaunch some products or services? Or eliminate them from your offering?

▷ Where are your products and your firm in their life cycles?

▷ Should you be taking specific actions?

▷ Are you monitoring performance?

Your marketing

▷ Are your marketing efforts worth the expense and the effort?

▷ What sort of ROI are you generating on your promotion and advertising campaigns?

▷ Have you reviewed your brand?

▷ Do you know what you want to achieve with it?

▷ Is your pricing correct?

▷ Does it achieve what you want in the marketplace?

▷ Are you taking advantage of everything the web has to offer?

▷ Are you investing in digital technology or just seeing it as an expense?

▷ Have you reviewed how your sell your product, where you sell and who to?

Complete the assessment

Reading through those questions may have prompted some ideas, maybe even some big ones. But as we have seen, every issue can be addressed in an achievable sequence. At the end of the movie *Superman*, Clark Kent was faced with the loss of Lois Lane. The only solution was to reverse the direction in which the earth was rotating, and to do so for as long as it would take to get back to a time prior to her demise. A pretty big ask you might say, and one requiring all of his somewhat remarkable skills. But what was the first thing he had to do? It was the same thing he always has to do ahead of doing everything else:

he had to find a phone box. Even Superman has to start with the first step.

So to stay in perpetual motion, find the next step. Table 51.1 will be familiar. It is the same as table 2.1, except the areas have been changed. The process is the same.

Rate yourself between 1 and 10 in each area. Look at where you want to be in each and compare it with reality. Choose the one where you feel you have the most to gain, then spend some quiet time imagining what it would be like to be there. Relax. Take your time. You won't be getting there today.

When you are ready, find your 'phone box'. Write down the very first step you have to take to move closer to achieving that goal. That's what you will do today, and that's all. Staying recharged can be that simple. Try driving home differently today.

Table 51.1: business balance assessment

Areas	Now (A)	Goal (B)	Rank (B – A)	Positives (your strengths in this area)	Action (the first step towards achieving your goal)
Yourself					
Your finances					
Your team					
Your firm					
Your marketing					

52
Remain recharged
Using the CASA principle

In August 1991, a virtually unknown technology student named Linus Benedict Torvalds sat before his computer in Helsinki, Finland. He posted a simple message on an online noticeboard. He said he was developing a free computer operating system and he wanted to know what features people thought it should have. At that time, operating systems were the domain of corporate heavyweights such as IBM and Microsoft. They were protected by extensive patents and backed by fierce commercial strategies.

By the turn of the millennium, Linux, as it came to be known, had emerged as a world-class operating system protected not by patent but by 'copyleft' (as opposed to copyright) under a licence that prevents it being used for commercial purposes.

Today, Linux powers everything from computers to mobile phones. Its success spurred the 'open source' movement, which now encompasses several hundred thousand such projects. Major software companies once opposed to it now use it. It continues to evolve today and thousands of programmers around the world contribute to it. In 2010, Torvald was listed as one of the 100 most influential inventors of all time.

Linux was not developed in the research and development department of a large corporation. It emerged through the cooperation of massive numbers of like-minded people. It is a key example used by Jeff Howe in *Crowdsourcing* to restate a fundamental but often overlooked truth about human beings:

> They can often be organized more efficiently in the context of community than … in the context of a corporation. The best person to do a job is the one who most wants to do that job.

This is reflected in what I call the 'CASA principle': four basic words that can turbocharge any idea. Apply them to your situation and you will achieve a result. It is not rocket science. It is simply a way forward that leads to action. CASA stands for 'collaboration, adaptation, simplification and action'. Start with the first.

Use the template in figure 52.1 (overleaf) to guide you through the CASA process. The logic behind collaborating, adapting, simplifying and acting have been woven throughout this book. Cross-references to various chapters are included so that you can review relevant topics as you work through this process.

Collaboration

Throughout this book we have stressed the leveraging power of working with others. Linux is just one example of this. Your own business is a function of collaboration—with your suppliers, your customers, your community and all the other stakeholders in that business. Your teamwork is a collaborative effort. So is your think tank. So is your marketing.

A second point made in *Crowdsourcing* is that people work best when they share a common objective. It's what they want to do. Just as a person's favourite activity reflects their strengths, collaborative effort is optimised when those strengths are applied to a common goal.

Businesses structures can get in the way of this essential truth. How often is marketing strategy left up to the marketing team? Or pricing policy left up to finance?

Figure 52.1: steps in the CASA process

Project name:	
Collaboration *Key questions:* • Who do I need to work with? • What strengths will we need? *The process:* Assemble the team. (Chapters 1, 2, 4, 9, 25, 26, 27, 28, 33, 34, 35, 48)	**Adaptation** *Key questions:* • What's changed? • What needs to be changed? *The process:* Develop the plan. (Chapters 7, 10, 19, 24, 30, 33, 36, 38, 39, 41, 42, 50, 51)
Simplification *Key questions:* • Is the plan achievable? • What steps need to be taken? *The process:* Plan the steps. (Chapters 2, 4 ,9, 17, 18, 30, 40, 51)	**Action** *Key questions:* • What is the first step? • Who will do what by when? *The process:* Take the first step. (Chapters 1, 2, 3, 50, 52)

Or product development left up to research and development? In an environment that is changing as rapidly as it is today, the failure to cross-fertilise the individual strengths within a business means failure to adapt to fundamental shifts in the market landscape.

The first question an active manager needs to ask when approaching any new initiative is: 'Who do I need to collaborate with to the make this happen?' Go back to our discussion on think tanks. They do not have to be composed only of people directly relevant to the task. It is essential to include people who want to work on the idea, including those whose only contribution is their keenness for idea development in general. It can, and possibly should, include people external to the business, such as suppliers and customers and in some cases even competitors.

In an informal weekend workshop back in the early days of Web 2.0, three people got together in a garage. One wrote manuals on how to use agricultural equipment. One printed the manuals. The other used them.

The writer wanted to find better ways of delivering manuals to the end-user. The printer wanted the writer's business. The user wanted an easily accessible alternative to manuals that got lost in the workshop. He also wanted clearer explanations of how to do certain things.

The result of this simple collaboration of a producer, a supplier and a customer was a basic website. They created it from freely available software. The printer turned a manual into an e-book. They shot a 90-second video, directed by the end-user, on how to handle a particular fitting. They uploaded the lot onto the site.

By Sunday afternoon, they had a prototype for a site where any number of manuals could be referenced. The writer would continue to write, the printer moved into e-books and website design, and the end-user could call up the manual anytime, from one source, together with a video of processes that were difficult to explain in writing.

It was a brief collaboration that led to a product with great potential. It didn't cost anything other than time. When asked about the project, they described it as 'a great weekend'. It was fun to do. They enjoyed the process. They were a diverse group. They all worked for different companies, their ages ranged from generation Y to baby boomer, and they had completely different skills and experience. What they had in common was an objective. It's a strong argument for the creative power of diversity.

Collaboration doesn't have to start in a garage. It can begin over lunch, in the boardroom or at a staff meeting. The next time you think of a new initiative, or face a new problem, start by asking three questions:

1   What strengths are required to develop this?
2   Who has them?
3   Who should I collaborate with?

This is the first step in the CASA process: assemble the team. The team will then develop the plan. You will then plan the steps. Then you will take the first one.

Adaptation

Once you have gathered the team, you will move on to adaptation. This raises another question: why do you have to do anything at all?

No business model is static. People change, markets shift, economies cycle and technology just keeps evolving. The environment in which you operate is in perpetual motion, even if you aren't. The challenge for the adaptive manager is not just to catch up if you have fallen behind. Staying current is hard enough, but the real goal is to move to the front and become the leader in your field.

That might sound daunting, but the reality is that most business innovation is a series of small changes rather than dramatic shifts in the way you operate. Firms that stay ahead do so by ongoing adaptation. By constantly focusing on what's changing, or what needs to be changed, they develop a culture of constant innovation.

Change can be threatening, but it can also be exciting and motivating. The chapters on surfing the economic cycle, coping with crises and examining where you are in the life cycle of your business all ask the same question: what are you going to do about it? How are you going to adapt? This is the real core of business development, and the key to sustainable, innovative and creative business models. You need to challenge yourself, your think tank, your team or your colleagues to constantly explore how to adapt positively to changing circumstances.

It may be that you will embark on a major strategic rethink of your business, but the journey will still require an achievable sequence of events. If you are defining an issue where you want to make change, begin with something simple. At the firm level, what needs to be changed in your customer relations, your packaging and your supply chain? Maybe you just need to rearrange your floor plan.

Even at a personal level, small changes can dramatically increase your productivity. Have you reviewed the job specification of your personal assistant? Is it structured to optimise your productivity and your assistant's? Effectively collaborating with your assistant can revolutionise your management performance.

There is, however, a caution. People do respond to good ideas, and brainstorming can be inspiring and motivating—but only if people can see how it can be achieved. This leads us to the third and essential part of the process: keeping it simple. Approach change enthusiastically, but focus on the doable—the small shifts that lead to long-term progress.

Simplification

The hurdle that most change projects have to jump over is complexity. Your team might generate the most innovative session when gathered around the whiteboard, but once they sit back and look at it, the plan can appear overwhelming.

Suddenly they realise what they themselves might be required to do. They notice that restructuring things may well move them to a place that is way outside their comfort zone—something that can fundamentally change their relationship with the business. This is unsettling at best and downright scary at worst. It is one reason why large strategy shifts are often stillborn. But it is also why gradual change has the power to move mountains.

If your enthusiasm for ideas has run away with either you or your team, it is time for a simple reality check: is the planned change achievable? We have said that if you are embarking on a change project, you need to choose something doable. But even after you have developed a plan to do that, you need to make sure the plan itself is achievable.

The only way to do that is to break it down into steps. This reduces the threatening nature of the project. What scares people—including you—is the height of the mountain they have to climb. If you break the project down into sections, the achievement of each step becomes a goal in itself. You are doing a series of climbs rather than attempting one massive ascent. Every person, including you, can start to see that they can do this. Instead of being a threatening process, it becomes a motivating exercise in which people are supported by a sense of achievement as they reach each goal.

So focus on the process rather than the outcome. In writing this book, I found the goal of producing 52 chapters overwhelming. When I made it my goal to write only one chapter, I was able to start. I stopped caring about the book and worked on the chapter in front of me. Eventually I had 52.

In chapter 9, we introduced the principles of William of Ockham and Vilfredo Pareto. In chapter 50, we applied them to an 80:20 analysis of what action would produce the quickest result. In working through the CASA principle, apply them to simplifying your change project.

If you have managed to simplify your plan, the next step is the easiest. There is no point in any innovative activity unless it ends with an action. You have defined the first step. Now you just have to take it.

Action

You are now back where this book began. In the opening paragraphs, we asked this question: what actually makes a business work well? Various theories offer answers to this, but there is no single formula for success. One approach seems to work for some businesses, but not for others. There are many great management ideas, but, it seems, not that many great managers. That is not because people lack skills or passion. Most managers have both. Otherwise they probably wouldn't be in the roles they are in. What happens more often is that perfectly capable people become preoccupied with the responsibility of management rather than the creativity of it. They are promoted because of their strengths, only to find they have no time to apply them.

Your first action was to reverse this. Look to where you have strengths and start working them. Acknowledge your weaknesses. Delegate that part of your job that someone else can do better to someone who actually does do it better. That's management. It's also the beginning of collaboration. You have already started to adapt your management structure to what can be done with the resources at hand. Working with others is the simplest, least-expensive and fastest way to generate momentum.

Throughout, you have been reminded of the need for simplicity. It doesn't matter whether you are struggling with working capital management or setting off on an entirely new marketing direction. Don't be overwhelmed by it. If you apply the CASA principle to any situation, you will bring together the resources you need. Having planned what needs to be changed, and having simplified the route map into short sections of clear road, you are ready to take the next step.

It is time to act. You can start right away.

Index